Revival's Symphony

A.B. Smithyman

RIVER
PUBLISHING

River Publishing & Media Ltd
Barham Court
Teston
Maidstone
Kent
ME18 5BZ
United Kingdom

info@river-publishing.co.uk

ISBN 978-1-908393-27-2
Printed in the United Kingdom
Cover design by www.SpiffingCovers.com

Let mercy lead, let love be the strength in your legs.
And every footprint that you leave, there will be a drop
of grace. If we could reach beyond the wisdom of this age,
into the foolishness of God, that foolishness will save ...
Let mercy lead.

(Rich Mullins: *Let Mercy Lead*)

Table of Contents

The fog and the parlour

There are few activities more cooperative than the writing of
history. The author puts his name brashly on the title page and the
reviewers rightly attack him for his errors and misinterpretations;
but none knows better than he how much his whole enterprise
depends on the proceeding labours of others.

(Christopher Hill: *The World Turned Upside Down*)

For just under fifty minutes, the young preacher had delivered a
passionate plea for people to get themselves right before their Maker.
His heartfelt sermon blended the directness of Jonathan Edwards'
homily, *Sinners in the hands of an angry God*, with the exquisite
framing of Charles Spurgeon's *Facing the wind*, and now in its closing
words, chaos ensued.

The preacher's final cry invited all who were listening to reflect
upon their lifestyles through the mirror found at the foot of the cross.
The response was beyond his imagination as a sacred atmosphere
descended upon the packed auditorium. A murmuring within the
crowd suddenly erupted into a thundering bellow of confessional
prayer, as men, women and children of all backgrounds rushed towards
the pulpit to find solace for their troubled hearts.

Huddled together with no regard for their self-image was a landscape
of souls, a living topography of bended knees and prostrate intercession.
Like after Edwards' famous sermon of 1741, there was a commonality
of brokenness and tears within this holy moment. Time stood still,
as the hand of God made its imprint on the soft surface of contrite,
worshipping hearts. This visible touch from heaven's throne room
would forever remain within the consciousness of everyone present.

The young preacher's own eyes filled with tears. In the space of
only four months he had been propelled into the public spotlight, as
his sermons became recognised within his home city and beyond.
It wasn't so long ago that his audience numbered in single figures,
as he pastored a handful of teenagers. Yet that scenario completely
changed, when he began a study of Charles Finney.

He had encouraged his youth group to examine in detail Finney's
winter lectures of 1834, hoping that these *Blueprints for revival* would
spark a move of God. Finney's challenge not to neglect prayer, social
care, family duties, the means of grace and the preaching of the Word,

indeed stirred a deep passion within hearts. Prayer times and home group meetings sprang up, becoming a collective chorus of intercession and study. Conversations began as teachers, families and friends noticed the changes taking place. Momentum built when other church members joined in, and soon there was a unified cry for revival's touch.

And then it happened.

At four o'clock on a Tuesday morning, a dense fog descended upon the city. This display of nature became a fearful manifestation, as people suddenly woke up to find their private spaces invaded by an inexplicable mist. A deep sense of reverence for something beyond their own universe started to fill them. Some broke down in tears whilst others ran outside attempting to make sense of this strange phenomenon. 'Is it a terrorist attack . . . a disaster . . . the end of the world?'

Questions filled the morning air in a strange waltz of chaos and bewilderment. Sleepy pyjama-clad people mingled in the streets with early risers wearing well-pressed suits, dancing through each conjecture, looking to their neighbours for assurance that all would be well. When the streets seemed empty of solutions, attention turned to the local news, but again without answers. It was then that voices began to be heard. Lovers of Christ articulated, just as the Apostle Peter did on the day of Pentecost, that 'this is that' which had been prayed for and yearned for.

That moment seemed a long time ago for the preacher in the auditorium – one hundred and twenty two days according to his diary. In those four months, his youth Bible study changed into sold-out 'revival' meetings. Each day was unique and beyond his wildest imagination, yet without fail there was always a response, a visible sign that his talk had hit the mark.

Yet the 'altar call' was a time of trepidation for the young man. Hours before each meeting he would be in prayer, pleading to God to overlook his human weakness. He took comfort from the story of a healing evangelist called Kathryn Kuhlman who knew her own frailty as she wept before each service. Her cries to heaven that Christ would look past her imperfection and heal everyone in the room, gave the preacher comfort as he faced his own secret demons.

The preacher's simple prayer, 'Less of me, and more of you, God', never quenched his fear that one day there would be no response because his mistakes had finally caught up with him. Today though, his prayers seemed to have been answered again, and the call at the end of the sermon was deemed a public success.

Walking off the platform, he headed towards the side exit door. Thoughts began to dart through his mind, 'Was the fog still there . . . had it lifted . . . become lighter?' Since the fog had settled upon the city, it had become a sign of revival, an indication that the hand of God was still on that place. 'How long will this last?' he questioned as he nervously turned the handle of the door that led to the outside world.

To his joy, the fog was still present, still as dense and mysterious as the day it first descended. He stepped into the mist, feeling the gentle moisture refresh his sweating brow. The door closed behind him as the sound of weeping and prayers were heard down the neighbouring street. It was a common sound now, the reverberation of souls feeling the embrace of their loving Father. He made a mental note of where the heavenly tones were coming from, as he made his way back home. Another day in his diary crossed off, one hundred and twenty three days to be exact.

* * * * *

Every weekend for about two years I played out variations of that storyline to the images of six historic heroes of faith hanging upon my living room wall. Mixing a concoction of old-time revival messages, I preached a sermon in an imaginary land, a collage of books read, preachers heard and videos watched. This storyline moulded my daily life, guiding my prayers and efforts to fulfil that dream. Although I never saw that imaginary world turn into actuality, my solace was that vision of a wondrous outbreak of God's transforming power.

We all have our own versions of revival: opinions and definitions that reflect our history, politics and theological preferences. It's a complex patchwork of different fabrics. Our images of a move of God can be shaped by particular world events or prominent figures. The books we read or choose not to read can mould a storyline in a certain direction. The edit, then re-edit of classic revival literature can encourage a line of thought that influences readers for years to come.

History is full of these complexities. The journal of George Fox, one of the founders of the Quaker movement, tells of faithful exploits and purposeful sacrifices. Yet it makes minimal reference to a co-founder and partner in the work due to their relational breakdown. The journal was constructed retrospectively, editing history and leaving readers unaware of the gaps in the story.

This reshaping of reality could also be said of the abridged journals of John Wesley. Depending upon the editor and year of publication, many mundane incidents have been erased from the storyline, diminishing our awareness of interconnected events.

When we listen, interpret and tell the story of revival, the narratives that we communicate are coloured by the lenses that we wear.

> Imagine you enter a parlour. You come late. When you arrive, others have long preceded you, and they are engaged in a heated discussion, a discussion too heated for them to pause and tell you exactly what it is about. In fact, the discussion had already begun long before any of them got there, so that no one present is qualified to retrace for you all the steps that had gone before. You listen for a while, until you decide that you have caught the tenor of the argument; then you put in your oar. Someone answers; you answer him; another comes to your defense; another aligns himself against you … The hour grows late. You must depart. And you do depart, with the discussion still vigorously in progress (Burke, 1973).

In the parlour of life, the story of revival has been long discussed with many opinions expressed and different experiences described. Arthur Wallis alluded to this ongoing conversation when he pointed out that we cannot see how the word 'revival' was used in the Bible, because it is not there. There are many suggestions and examples, but nothing definite that can provide a 'full stop' to the debate.

So how do we approach such a diverse topic, while appreciating the worth of each contributor within the body of Christ? What we shape as our revival hope affects how we pray and work towards it on our own journey. I don't pretend to have the definitive answer, but want to throw an idea into this ongoing dialogue within life's parlour. It comes from within the four walls of my lounge, where a solitary performance was given to six hanging pictures.

The private sermons that I delivered were heavily influenced by Finney's winter lectures of 1834. His series of talks are among the most famous of revival narratives, and chapter titles such as *How to promote a revival* suggest a blueprint for starting and maintaining a work of God. I embraced this assumption and followed that blueprint in my own desire for God to move. Yet in their original context, those lectures take on a different meaning, far from the strict design that I had assumed.

Lawyer-turned-minister Finney travelled through the valleys and mountaintops of a revival experience. He walked amid the chaos of new teachings and expressions that challenged many long-held beliefs while respecting the traditions that had provided strong and valued foundations over the years. In a society where order was of the utmost value, he allowed the Gospel message to rock his own preferences, and shared his journey of mistakes and successes through his lectures.

These were not an exclusive platform for one man to share his beliefs and opinions. Instead, Finney attempted to give examples and signposts to further his own walk, and that of others around. He encouraged all to find ways of respectfully stepping into rhythm with the Holy Spirit without stifling His work. Knowing that a veil would inevitably cloud his vision, he humbly attached a preface.

> I wish the brethren to understand that I lay no claim of infallibility upon this subject. I only wish to give my opinions with that modesty which becomes my ignorance, and which is demanded also by the nature of the subject (Finney, 1979).

Purposely inviting dialogue, Finney created a space for ministers, parents and students to bring their own life experiences into an active discourse of exploration. These famous lectures were a living debate, trying to grasp hold of something that was already acknowledged as being unobtainable, but approached in the humility of learning and listening as each pilgrim shared their life story.

It's a beautiful and challenging approach which I seek to emulate within this book. An attempt to capture the awe of heaven's handprint upon the land of history, yet respectfully acknowledge that we know only in part. I pray that the following pages do justice to the intricate 'living symphony' of revival, a movement of love between the Lord of creation and creation itself.

The intricate living symphony

Symphony: An elaborate musical composition. Something regarded, typically favourably, as a composition of different elements.

(Oxford English Dictionary)

Imagine rising to your feet to applaud the conclusion of Dvorak's Symphony No. 9 in E minor. The 19th century composer has taken you on an exquisite forty-minute voyage of joyful discovery. Each of its four movements invites engagement with the complexity of its composition. One minute the gentle tones of a solitary instrument embrace your heart with delicate care, and the next a *fortissimo*, loud then soft dynamic, breaks through with effervescent vibrancy.

A smile appears on your face as you play back a section of the second movement in your mind which recalls a tune heard as a child (a bread-makers advert). There is a satisfied moment of recognition of that particular passage. The rolling waves of tonality continue crashing around the boat of your senses as you take hold of the programme notes and make your way towards the exit. You go home, eager to investigate this piece of music that stirred such a flow of emotions.

Searching the digital highway, it doesn't take long to discover more. Antonin Leopold Dvorak, the Czech composer, had been unable to refuse the opportunity in 1892 to work in America. The following year he produced this symphony, influenced by the Native Americans and their constant adaptations of their melodies, writings and folk songs. Echoing their values, Dvorak hoped that his own music would inspire continual change throughout the years to come.

This was soon realised as one of his students, William Fisher, wrote a choral arrangement to the theme of the second movement. The song called *'Goin' Home'* took on a life of its own, with many diverse interpretations. Some saw it as an anthem for the issue of race, whilst others approached it as a heartfelt spiritual song. It broke into the consciousness of a whole nation when it became associated with the funeral of the 32nd President of the United States of America, Franklin D. Roosevelt.

The multiple adaptations of the New World Symphony are staggeringly diverse works of music, literature and art, intertwined in a creative and evolving dance. All express the uniqueness of the author's hand, yet with common and unifying strands. It takes us on a journey of connections and influences, a participatory story of interpretation. When we hear the familiar sounds of the symphony once again, it is with a new-found appreciation of its intricate history.

* * * * *

I understood this idea of an evolving collaboration in one of the most moving experiences I have ever had. On an island off the coast of Scotland, I visited a man who had lived through the chapters of a revival storyline, the 'before,' 'during,' and 'afterwards.' Before our meeting I had already studied this famous move of God, the Hebrides Revival, focusing on characters such as the famous praying old ladies, Christine and Peggy Smith, and James Murray Mackay who had invited the preacher, Duncan Campbell, to join in.

The year 1949 became a pivotal year for that island, as Campbell would later describe:

> You met God on meadow and moorland; you met him in the homes of the people. God seemed to be everywhere . . . not an evangelist, not a special effort. Not anything at all based upon human endeavour, but an awareness of God that gripped the whole community so much so that work stopped (Smithyman, 2013).

During our precious conversations and times in prayer, this old man revealed a new complexity to the story I thought I knew. New characters were introduced, as well as different locations and dates around the time of the outpouring. The neatly boxed piece of history within my head was replaced with a stage platform being revealed by a curtain that was slowly being pulled back. Lost in wonder, I marvelled at the interplay of collaboration that went beyond the confines of a famous prayer, sermon and date of outpouring.

A few years after that meeting, this gentleman experienced the ultimate embrace of his Father, but the passing away of his life and the subsequent activities of my busy calendar have never diminished the memory of our conversation. In my bookshelves and note collections, I have an ever-expanding library of varied revival interpretations. Some can unify a group of people; others can cause disruption. Even my cherished heroes of faith display diverse conclusions and focal points

Some suggest a sovereign outpouring, while others lean towards a co-operation between God and his people. One person's revival tent meeting is another person's charismatic party. A social action movement for some is seen as a sign of sacrificial compassion, to others it is an overlooked element of revival.

There seems to be a never ending composition of thoughts and insights. All the storytellers' experiences of faith are valuable, yet they can also have contradictory viewpoints. Although there are different paths, behind the assortment of words, practice and theology there is a harmony in each pilgrim's journey of faith. To ask, 'Who is right and who is wrong?' is not a helpful way to grapple with a topic that is in essence, indescribable.

In that old man's living room, I sensed how elaborate the revival symphony could be. The word symphony, means 'a composition of different elements,' from the Greek root meaning 'harmonious and agreement.' It is a complex piece of work made up of diverse tones, expressed through many different types of instruments.

Although each note is carefully written down, the composer, musician and listener are all invited to bring their personal interpretations. The force of a bow, the fluidity of a finger upon the keys and the preferences of an individual, contribute to a piece of music that is at the same time historic and living, static and moving.

A bar of music might produce a short and magnificent melody, and its individual notes might resound with simple beauty. Yet when that measure is placed within the larger manuscript, it takes on a whole new life. This re-creation astounds the imagination, as those few notes become unified with everything around. There's an intimate interconnection between the note, musician, hearer and composer. It's a creative continuation as the part is combined with the whole, and then the whole becomes a part of something more.

In the musical scale there is structured freedom. For example, there are the melodic and harmonic scales, with their seven distinct notes, then the diatonic scale, with five whole steps, two half steps, and six notes of the whole tone. Beyond that is the Phrygian dominant scale with its unique key signatures. Its adaptations of the interval called the 'blue note' was made famous as a recording label offering 'uncompromising expressions . . . that represent an authentic way of musical feeling.' This ordered chaos and creative adaptation is exemplified in the musical world of jazz.

All scales have clear ground rules without being exclusive. Notes are laid down in specific formats, but are open for re-imagination and intimate participation. There is unity within their diversity.

This attempt to grapple with the indefinable leads me to consider how the created and the Creator dance so intimately in the space called a revival. It is an intricate interaction of diverse tones and textures beyond the realms of any created lexicon. We define such moments through the lens of our beliefs, preferences and personal experiences, but by putting them in some theological scale could cause us to miss the wider manuscript that these bars are a part of.

There is a beautiful vulnerability in this picture that is to be welcomed. Revival is an enigma that we don't have exclusive rights to define; we certainly don't have the one and only hotline to heaven's logic. Instead, we have snippets of God's one true creative manuscript, carrying heavenly notes to be played. These phrases lead us to the next measure of music, taking us on a whole new journey of experience.

It is tempting to try to make sense of this complexity. Yet we must humbly recognise that our tidy scale will never fully describe revival's beauty. It is instead a mere interpretation of a few bars of heaven's music that is indefinable by earthly logic, notes of creative simplicity and harmonious complexity that is being played through the lives of pilgrims of our faith.

This intricate living symphony is eloquently described through the words of a worshipful psalm,

> *God is magnificent; He can never be praised enough. There are no boundaries to his greatness. Generations after generations stand in awe of your work; each one tell stories of your mighty acts. Your beauty and splendour have everyone talking . . .*
>
> *I could write a book full of the details of your greatness. The fame of your goodness spreads across the country; your righteousness is on everyone's lips.*
>
> (Psalm 145:3-7 *The Message*)

Note 'C'
Storytelling tradition

Introduction: What makes a good story?

> There are parts of me in every character, male and female
> that I've written. There have to be. You have to get
> your blood in there somehow.

(Aaron Sorkin: Interview in *The Telegraph* 15th October 2010)

'Marley was dead, to begin with. There is no doubt whatever about that.' From the opening line of Charles Dickens' *A Christmas Carol*, the story rocked social conventions of Victorian Britain. Tales of this wintery season were supposed to focus upon the state encouraged festive gatherings, not lead the reader to consider the evils of a harsh businessman and the ideology that his character represented. Yet it soon won critical acclaim, warranting a reprint and numerous creative retellings. People were intrigued by the story of Scrooge, a cruel tycoon who was visited by his dead business partner on the night of Christmas Eve. Marley, who carried in death chains that were crafted during his life, warned Scrooge that he was destined for the same fate if he rejected the visit of three separate ghosts. They would appear as guides, leading him to visit his past, present and future.

Although this is the story of one man's redemption, it also carried a pointed social message. When selfish Scrooge was asked for donations to go towards the poor over Christmas, he likened his view of charity to that of the Poor Law of 1834, which funnelled any state help through the harsh conditions of the workhouse. This was not a loose comment from the author, but a pointed observation. The law was a contentious topic of the day, provoking many debates about whether this was a cost cutting exercise for the rich and middle class while the poor were pushed to one side. As Scrooge made his way 'along the crowded paths of life, warning all human sympathy to keep its distance,' the reader could not avoid the deeper message. Scrooge was not just a man but an ideology, paying little attention to those in need.

Then Scrooge saw his old partner's face on the front door knocker. With a sense of dread he ventured into his rooms. He stared at his fireplace, and noted the Biblical characters that decorated the surround, while recalling the face of Marley. Ringing bells and the clanking of chains were heard in the distance, warning the reader to expect a message of utmost importance from the ghost who was likened to a prophetic rod. The journey through Scrooge's past was not just about the hardening of his own heart, but a prophetic statement about the society of the day and its future. A mirror held up to reveal the fruit of self-centred choices – the inner children of 'want' and 'ignorance'.

Through the visitation of the three ghosts, Scrooge was faced with the harsh reflection of his heart, he cried out,

> I am not the man I was ... I will live in the past, the present, and the future. The Spirits of all three shall strive within me. I will not shut out the lessons that they teach (Dickens, 1922).

Scrooge was a reformed man, yet in the closing scene the author delivers one final stroke. In a society where disability was treated harshly by the law and social opinion, a crippled boy takes centre stage. Welcomed into the arms of Scrooge, this child declares, 'God bless us every one!' Scrooge, who represented a political and social ideology, now takes on the sacrificial role of fatherhood. Charles Dickens is making a direct and unabashed call to love one's neighbour as oneself.

A Christmas Carol may not carry the impact now that it once did within the 19th century, but it continues to knock at the heart of humanity. It was written in the context of one of the greatest movements of social activism and religious awakening Great Britain has ever seen. Victorian men and women, organisations and people movements preached the gospel message with actions as well as words. Regardless of gender, wealth, status or education, there was a concerted movement of heartfelt compassion as followers of Christ grappled with the injustices of their society.

Some demonstrated this love through business, others through church-led projects, charitable structures and evangelistic crusades. It was as if a mighty stream from heaven's throne room was rushing through the veins of a nation's history. As pilgrims burned with the fire of an awakened conscience, each one shone the message of salvation and Christ's love into the dark corners of their world through their unique abilities, gifting and dreams.

Today, some of those initiatives may seem flawed when viewed in critical hindsight. But such varied forms of service created a foundation for many of the charitable and social constructs we cherish today. From education to the care for the wounded and destitute, to the development of child support and family investment, no aspect of society was left untouched. This love-led response communicated the revival message through a rainbow of hues.

In these dynamic tales of activism and crowded crusade meetings there is a beautifully diverse display of creativity. From a printed word to a dance on a stage, from a song composed to a reading of poetry, the author and performer tapped into a message running deep into the heart of a nation.

This communication was not just confined to the Victorian period. The bards and minstrels of the day were those who conveyed God's heartbeat through their own created works. Whether enjoyed by millions or simply appreciated within the intimacy of a fire-lit lounge, the Holy Spirit was filtering through each phrase.

William Williams wrote the treasured hymn *Bread of Heaven*. During the 18th century revival in Wales, he saw the need to convey the story of faith in his native tongue. Religious terminology was limited at this time due to the discriminatory exposure and stature of education. So building upon the learning revolution that Griffith Jones and the Society of Promoting Christian Knowledge had spearheaded, he framed a poetic story that amplified the revival message of famous preachers such as Daniel Rowland.

In 1,451 verses of poetry called *Theomemphus*, Williams crafted a tale of faith in everyday language that took the reader on a journey of conviction, repentance and practical discipleship. Despite others' disapproval of his directness about human guilt and temptation, Williams completed his work. Mirroring the honesty and vulnerability found in the Psalms, it would later be recognised as a giant of spiritual literature.

Our gaze could also fall upon John Milton and his masterpiece *Paradise Lost*, which is more than just a description of spiritual realms. This acclaimed work was a social and political commentary, speaking creatively of the religious uprising that was taking place within the country during the English Civil War. Though this battle was about royalty and its domain, it was also a movement of people who had been stirred by being able to access Scripture in their own language.

People began to articulate controversial themes such as the 'Inner Light'. This idea that God spoke directly within your heart without the means of mediation, challenged the structure of both priest and king. When mixed with the tensions of oppression and distribution of wealth, an uprising emerged that truly did turn England upside down.

Milton, like many others, interpreted these events as Christ's kingdom being at hand, believing that the actions of believers would finally usher in Jesus' return. Through bloodshed and violence a new seat of power was erected, and sadly, very soon many saw their hopes lost and the very thing they fought against reappearing in another form.

Paradise Lost and *Bunyan's Pilgrims Progress* in differing ways took up these themes. The authors crafted the arguments, agendas, success, failures and dreams of the day into narratives that held nuggets of treasured values as well as warnings. These were not just storylines to please readers' emotions, but wisdom articulated in a way that propelled the faith further – radical ideas that combined spiritual development with the pursuit of equality and justice.

These are but a few examples of spiritual messages which were amplified into homes that the pulpit could never reach. From classical composers to painters and songwriters, history records an endless display of salvation messages. Although the artists may have been flawed, their God-given imagination produced a miraculous symphony. The marvellous prism of creativity truly does shine the wavelengths of his message through these colourfully crafted stories.

A strange partnership

The artist brings something into the world that didn't exist
before, and ... he does it without destroying something else.

(George Plimpton: *Writers at Work*)

It was 1762, and a developing scandal captivated the attention of the
city of London. Before an avid audience, the news streams and gossip
undercurrents relayed the storyline of a love affair, a murder, a court
case and the unknown realms of the supernatural that were unfolding
from 33 Cock Lane. Because this incident involved a series of séances
where a ghost accused a member of the public with murder, it raised
the question on whether a public investigation was warranted.

This frenzied saga was debated in some of the highest circles of
society. Eventually an eminent committee was set up to investigate
the allegations of murder, including a lord, a bishop, a doctor and Dr.
Samuel Johnson, author of the groundbreaking dictionary of the
English language. There was even a highly publicised visit to the grave
of the deceased.

Finally fraud was discovered and the main culprit was sent to
prison. This bizarre story that was nicknamed the 'Cock Lane Ghost'
filled the press and was discussed everywhere, from slum dwelling to
mansion house. It even crept into sermon topics of many pulpits.

One such pulpit was of an emerging group called the Methodists.
This band of travelling preachers and local congregations had shaken
the foundations of religion as they embraced the power of Scripture
for the betterment of society, blending the call for salvation with a
radical pursuit for justice. Not willing to be tied down to convention,
their evangelistic work carried a pioneering edge and their blend of
spirituality and activism tapped into the issues of the day. Whether it
was about family support, education, employment, social disorder or
drunkenness, their work reflected the talking points of the street – and
it seemed natural to pick up on the city's biggest news story in 1762.

The Methodists wanted to encourage people to consider the realm
of the supernatural, particularly the fate of the soul after death. Reports
are varied, but the events at Cock Lane proved a timely opportunity for
them to further personal reflection. Some members, despite disagreeing
with the operation of séances, supported the spiritual business venture
that was being run from the ghostly house, hoping that it would provide

a platform for worried hearts to connect to the Methodist work and the message of repentance. Other accounts tell of how other members crafted sermons and tracts about the broader topics of the story, such as debt, honesty and justice.

One artistic commentary on these unfolding events could appear as a direct attack on the most prominent figure of Methodism, John Wesley. The artist certainly had little respect for the preacher's interpretation of the Christian faith. Yet his work displayed a peculiar unity in its mocking, a partnership that highlights how diverse the revival message can be.

In a painting called *The Sleeping Congregation*, William Hogarth lampooned the effects and immoral contradictions of an Anglican sermon in 1736. He followed this with *Credulity, Superstition, and Fanaticism* which now questioned the more controversial practices of the Methodist movement.

Hogarth set the scene in one of their 'meeting houses', suggesting that they were anything but sacred places. Many individuals are depicted as being caught up in fervent displays of worship and wild enthusiasm, and apparently fainting under the power of God. A disguised Methodist preacher is hiding his Catholic background, dressed up as a harlequin with allusions to money by his head, while the preacher acts as a puppeteer, dangling images of death and the journey beyond the grave before the terrified congregation. To question the use of the supernatural, a thermometer measuring the emotional temperature in the room rests on a book of Wesley's, alongside a minister placing an icon of the Cock Lane ghost down the front of a lady's dress.

Hogarth was sneered at by some as a comic painter whilst others held him in highest esteem, but his works graced daily newspapers as well as prestigious galleries around the world. His narrative style meant that 'his graphic representations were indeed books: they had the teeming, fruitful, suggestive meaning of words.' He found creative channels of distribution that bypassed the usual means of control, so many could access these images of social commentary.

One such narration was Hogarth's six paintings and engravings called *A Harlot's Progress*. They told the story of a young woman's journey of seduction into prostitution and the sad demise of her life. In storyboard fashion, it highlighted the harsh reality of life, the ignorance of observers around and the ineffectiveness of religious organisations. Hogarth invited any who gazed at the images to 'play an active part in the realisation of the work and devise their own course within it.'

His painting, *Gin Lane*, depicted the depravity of the inner city slums ravaged by drunkenness; his series, *Four Stages of Cruelty*, graphically showed the destructive path of anger; while *Industry and Idleness* was a call to embrace the ethics of hard work. Hogarth attempted to convey the moral bankruptcy of the day, and challenged society to respond. He challenged religious groups to live out the sermons they preached, and not to cross to the other side of the road when human beings were in need.

Hogarth's work upset many, including John Wesley and the Methodist movement. They were often considered in opposition to each other, yet paradoxically they were on the same path. A trail of faith that provoked the conscience of a nation, and one in which their lives refused to let anyone easily off the hook.

Thoughts

The world has become a strange and puzzling place that keeps insisting I give up what I thought I knew. I don't expect to ever again feel secured by intellectual confidence, but I find life much more interesting now living with not knowing, trying to stay curious rather than certain.

(Margaret Wheatley)

By studying history, we can use hindsight as a tool to appreciate the value of partnerships. Seen from a distant viewpoint, we can see how the interplay of diverse characters, decisions and moments all contribute to the whole. What may not have looked like a unified operation at the time is in fact a staggering performance of diversity.

In their day, Wesley and Hogarth seemed like two opposing forces. They rejected each other's efforts, identifying the other's faults and considering them enemies. Nevertheless, both characters were passionate for the cause of righteousness, and both interpreted their work through the lens of faith, whether changing the law on the consumption of gin, the establishment of such projects as the Foundling Hospital that took care of unwanted children, or the pursuit and promotion of a spiritual revolution. In fact, they were both dancing to the currents of the one true Spirit, a duet between God and humanity.

This dynamic is common to the pilgrimage of faith, one that every lover of Christ travels. Where footprints of devoted service are entwined in heart-felt vision, but its union with fellow travellers are clouded by our preferences and theological stance.

There are no easy answers, but we must embrace our journey like that of a child and be captivated by the life-stories unfolding right before our eyes. Curiosity disrupts tunnel vision that passions can so easily construct. Our inquisitiveness hears the words of faithful service that sing from the lips of diverse travelling companions.

This heavenly medley is a patchwork of colourful acts of devotion that blanket the path of life that we travel. The choice is very clear. We can focus on one small piece of cloth or gaze upon the collective design. The synthesis of God's own needlework continually created through the participation of many hands.

It's all in a story

Stories don't always end where their authors intended,
but there is joy in following them, wherever they take us.

(Beatrix Potter: *Miss Potter*)

Once upon a time there were two storytellers who had witnessed the harsh reality of life. For both characters this was no fairytale or imaginary landscape, as the scars on their memories bore witness to injustice and pain. One was a storyteller of exceptional writing ability, the other a more simple soul: yet both danced to a grass-roots spiritual movement that was shaking the very core of a nation's conscience.

Charles Dickens was born February 1812. Because his father had a respectable clerk's job, he anticipated an academic education. But when the family became in debt to a retailer for forty pounds and ten shillings, society harshly turned its back on them. At the age of twelve, the young Dickens' world was turned upside down as his father and family members were imprisoned in the notorious debtor's prison on the South Bank of the River Thames, called Marshalsea.

Inmates were required to feed and clothe themselves. Occasionally through kind-hearted wardens or charitable initiatives, bread and water was supplied, but a corrupt black-market and protection racket teemed in the cells and guardrooms alike. This harsh system was designed to be a deterrent, while bringing profit to the prison corporation. The dreadful sting in its tail was the slow death by starvation for those who fell within its cracks.

While Charles' family was behind the prison's dark walls, he worked to help pay off the debt and provide the bare essentials of clothing and food. His exposure to warehouse work at such a young age remained with him for the rest of his life. Menial tasks in harsh conditions at the blacking factory near Charing Cross mocked his earlier dreams of education and stature. As he worked long hours in a rat-infested, broken-down building, the promising foundation of his life now seemed to be shattered.

Charles' childhood was stolen away through no fault of his own. Over time the family debt was paid, and normality returned, but his heart was scarred by shame and bitterness. He sacrificed playtime to work and carved out time to learn shorthand and varied writing styles. With a friend's help he eventually became a freelance reporter, and then a writer of vivid stories that captured his readers' imagination. At the launch of his periodical, *Household Words*, Dickens explained his mission – that 'no mere utilitarian spirit' would quash the heart: he would not be held back from declaring what he both observed and felt within.

Dickens' works can now be found in our libraries and bookshops and displayed on television and even cinema screens. His literature has been praised around the entire world, having a deep influence upon the lexicon of the English language: no one who has lived in the past two hundred years has come close to the amount of citations used within the Oxford English Dictionary.

The stories he penned are admired as literary masterpieces, but they are also radical social critiques, purposefully constructed to provoke change. For example, his novel *Little Dorrit* provoked a national debate on the Marshalsea prison. The adjective 'Dickensian' was later coined for squalid and poverty-stricken environments because of his astute use of fictional characters to highlight the issues of the day.

Dickens' faith was very important to him, as an Anglican he saw the Christian's responsibility as beyond the pew. He struggled with personal failings but found solace in using his writing ability as well as engaging in social action. He invested in a rehabilitation centre for vulnerable women, and supported a radical work later called the Great Ormond Street Hospital for Sick Children. He helped the educational reform movement, Ragged Schools, promoting the cause through novels such as *Oliver Twist*.

In partnership with the sanitation reformer, Edwin Chadwich, Dickens wrote provocative stories about the need for clean water and contained sewerage. They were based on the shocking 'Ghost Map' compiled by the physicist John Snow and a local vicar called Henry Whitehead, which showed the impact of untreated water in the poorest areas of the city. His themes married justice with the creative arts, touching on the abolition of slavery and the protection of the vulnerable. Dickens' narratives were designed to bring the darkness of the street alleyways into brightly lit, warm homes all across the country.

The second storyteller was Rebecca Jarrett, born in 1846 to a family of seven children. When the father passed away, they were soon struggling with little means of support. Although the other children were sent to work, Rebecca's mother ensured that she had access to a school education; nevertheless as a 10-year-old girl she had to balance school life with bringing her mother home from heavy drinking bouts.

At the age of thirteen she escaped being raped by a seventy-year-old man, but soon turned to drink herself. Her life became a never-ending maze of dead ends, as her habit demanded both her body and her purse. With her mother still under her care, prostitution became her means of survival, exposing her to the city's wretched underbelly.

Rebecca eventually crossed paths with an officer from the Salvation Army, and was taken to a London Rescue Home in 1885. The recounting of her tragic life story to the co-founder of The Salvation Army, Catherine Booth, represented the hidden lives of girls being trafficked and treated as slaves within the streets of the capital. Her raw portrayal of abuse could not be ignored, but within the same year a series of events led to her standing in the dock, accused of abduction and indecent assault.

She, along with a number of individuals including Bramwell Booth and a controversial journalist called William Thomas Stead, recognised an opportunity to reignite the interest in The Criminal Law Amendment Act that had become stuck between the Houses of The Commons and the Lords for the last three years. Their *spark* was to purchase a thirteen-year-old girl called Eliza Armstrong from a previously convicted alcoholic mother. They drugged the young girl and placed her in a brothel, waiting for her first client to appear. The client was Stead himself, pretending to be a 'punter' to demonstrate how a young girl could be trafficked for the sum of five pounds. Eliza was instead handed over to the Salvation Army to be placed in paid employment with a new family across the sea in France.

Stead had agreed to write a series of provocative newspaper articles that included the chronicles of how brave volunteers posed as prostitutes, punters and brothel keepers, risking their own safety to expose the reality behind closed doors. His final piece in *The Maiden Tribute of Modern Babylon*, recounted the purchase of Eliza. It was to be the climax of a strategy directed at the heart of a nation, and it lived up to its hopes.

The scheme caused shock and outrage within the high courts of power and the slums of inner cities. The players were charged and stood trial, with Jarrett and Stead serving six and three months respectively. Although their means of activism were questioned due to how they had originally manipulated the mother of Eliza into selling her daughter (which in her mind was for maid duty only), alongside the young girls pitiful aftercare in France, they did raise awareness of the cause, spearheading a final push to see the age of consent raised through the Criminal Law Amendment Act of 1885.

Rebecca continued to be an active worker of the Salvation Army. She experienced the joy of seeing lives changed, as well as facing the full force of mobs chasing her down with sticks and stones. She summed up her life,

> Here I am 40 years since I first entered the Salvation Army Home in Hanbury Street. A poor drunken broken-up woman, Mrs. Gen. and Mrs. Bramwell Booth did not look at that side. I was degraded, sunken down low by drink. Their work was to try and raise me up. They first got me into the hospital where I was kept 10 weeks to defeat the old devil drink.

> Today I have defeated the devil drink for 39 years. Here I am living amongst those, who like myself once, are fighting the drink. I pray each day for God to help me I am now nearing my other Home. I'm near 79 years in age but I am closing my earthly life with sincere gratitude to the Salvation Army and the precious officers for their care and devotion to me (Salvation Army Heritage Centre).

Rebecca's painful story contributed to a series of events that not only provided healing for herself but for countless others. Women of all ages and backgrounds found their hidden plight now in the open, being discussed around the dinner tables and the seats of governmental power. Rebecca never forgot the dark backstreets, but telling her own story has resulted in safety for many today.

Dickens' use of serials and cliff-hangers paved the way for a new form of mass story telling. Readers flocked to get the next update while their consciences were stirred about the evils in their society. The diverse storylines contributed to a wider narrative of grass root social reform, a realm of activism being outworked by countless pilgrims of faith.

Dickens and Jarrett, alongside many others, contributed to a work that was greater than that of just one individual. From mass readership to the intimacy of one-to-one conversations, their tones of narrative slipped past the hardest barriers and soaked the fertile ground being tilled by the Spirit's hand. They watered the seeds of conscience and action, and brought forth a nourishing harvest for those who needed it the most.

Thoughts

> And the first question that the priest asked; the first question that the Levite asked was, 'If I stop to help this man, what will happen to me?' But then the Good Samaritan came by, and he

reversed the question. 'If I do not stop to help this man,
what will happen to him?' That's the question before you tonight.
Not 'If I stop to help the sanitation workers, what will happen
to my job?' Not, 'If I stop to help the sanitation workers what will
happen to all of the hours that I usually spend in my office
every day and every week as a pastor?' The question is not,
'If I stop to help this man in need, what will happen to me?'
The question is, 'If I do not stop to help the sanitation workers,
what will happen to them?' That's the question.

(Martin Luther King, Jr: *I've Been to the Mountaintop*)

The parable of the Good Samaritan is a story that has forever remained with me from Sunday school of my childhood. I was struck by the tale of an injured man who needed help, yet people passed him by and left him for dead. Then a show of compassion by the person least expected, was a lesson to us all that 'loving your neighbour', means practical help for those we don't know.

As I grew up I was exposed to the differing interpretations of such a parable. Was it a reference to Jesus and the lost, a critique of religious expressions? Was it a political commentary, using the provocative imagery of a Jewish man needing help from the opposition? Theological assessments and ethical statements were brought to bear on this story of practical love. Yet I am reminded of the simplicity of this story once again, as I consider the lives of Charles Dickens and Rebecca Jarrett.

The traveller had ventured on a road that some called 'the way of blood.' It was a dangerous trail, one not travelled lightly, full of hideaways for thieves and gangs to pounce on any unsuspecting individual, taking goods and leaving their living 'cash machine' dazed and in fear. So the traveller succumbed, unable to move and with his life draining away.

A Priest and a Levite each passed by, both respectable and with a religious status that suggested closeness with Almighty God. Yet neither stopped, instead ensuring they walked the other side of the path.

I have often wondered why they did that. Was it fear, not knowing whether the robbers were still there? Or as Martin Luther King Jr. suggested, were they thinking more of themselves than the need? Either way, it challenges me about the fine line between being unaware and wilfully ignorant. One can be blind to something, not even giving thought to a situation, or deliberately choosing not to see or engage. A 'get-out clause' is not asking certain questions, to deny knowledge and free one's conscience.

It can be painful to observe how much of one's focus on the world is through the lens of self-interest. This selfishness is expressed in many ways, and is all too evident in my own life and actions. I observe so much injustice around me, yet filter my response through a series of internal questions and rationalising. My track record is not that good, and rarely touches the heights of the Samaritan. Yet I take encouragement from the lives of these storytellers, who demonstrate the power of narration.

They teach me that compassion takes many forms, and no expression of love takes precedence over another. All of them face the challenge of choosing between self and a stranger's need. Help to the traveller in the famous parable comes from an unexpected hero: someone who not only acts on the spot but follows up with a personal investment of time and resources.

Charles and Rebecca could be seen as unexpected heroes in a revival narrative, choosing not to ignore the situation they witnessed firsthand. Although they expressed their engagement differently, a beautiful commonality shone through their actions. The act of storytelling is not merely verbal; it is a demonstration of love that guides a response.

A proactive day of rest

I have always thought the actions of men the best
interpreters of their thoughts.

(John Locke: *An Essay Concerning Human Understanding*)

The rough seas of enlightened debate had troubled the sometimes vague and elusive faith statements of the 19th century. The rolling waves of turbulent water challenged all who considered themselves brave and intrepid travellers to explore the unknown and re-examine what was truth. Sermons that had once captured the hearts of a crowd were now under the microscope of intense scrutiny, examining each phrase in the light of rational review.

This was not the first time that the fragile relationship of logic and faith had been challenged. A century earlier, the spiritual and superstitious beliefs of society were being critiqued. Scientists, theorists, artists and commentators all called people to take hold of their own destiny through the advancement of knowledge. They demanded that human beings not be held captive by the chains of oppressive thought and imperialistic statements.

Religious beliefs and ancient traditions were particularly in the firing line, which naturally caused concern within the camps of the faithful. Yet many of these fears were allayed as people began to appreciate the opportunities to question and explore. The Enlightenment caused us to grapple in heated debate about faith and science, religion and the creative arts, producing a synergy of thought that no-one had originally expected. Yet now things had moved on.

As the students of enlightenment created their own definitions of reason, religious practices once again came under critical examination. Navigating through these storms were characters like Charles Grandison Finney and the 'Prince of Preachers' Charles Haddon Spurgeon. Their captivating sermons echoed the debating style of the day; each was robust and well-articulated, carrying academic weight.

Although they praised coherent thought, like the French minister in George Bernanos' novel *Diary of a Country Priest*, they saw that "reason will always obscure what we wish to keep in the shadows." They launched into the key debates of the day, provoked by the challenges of faith-led living. Their freedom of expression and rationality was respected in many quarters. As they declared their beliefs, they also embraced the pursuit of self-challenge that reflected the heartbeat of the Enlightenment.

Whether it was Finney's daring encouragement of women to pray in meetings, or the development of the anxious seat (sinner's prayer) that combined personal salvation with social activism, his questioning of accepted traditions brought advancement.

Spurgeon was also willing to question tradition. His missionary work blended social responsibility with the power of the creative arts, and brought fresh imagination to evangelism. As foundations of traditional thought were being rocked from all quarters, their endeavours were deemed radical and dangerous, particularly for those who struggled to balance on the tightrope of questions and exploration.

These two heroes of the evangelical faith were not the only ones to explore aspects of faith. Their voices merged with the undercurrents of advancement of learning and reason.

One such ripple was expressed through an Irishman by the name of Thomas Campbell, who was articulating thoughts about the apostolic nature of the church. A student of the philosopher John Locke (who was seen as an enemy of the church by many within Christendom), Campbell took the themes of liberalism, knowledge through experience and religious tolerance, and challenged the rationale for statements of faith such as the creed. Motivated by a passion for unity and religious freedom, he believed that Scripture was robust and clear enough for people to engage with themes of faith in their own way.

His daring political statements about church and state crossed both sides of the Atlantic, producing waves of disturbance about the role of priestly mediation. But most provocative was his suggestion that faith was more than an internal decision or repeated phrase. He argued that the creed was a living and active entity, an evolving statement of life to be shaped by each believer outworking their faith.

A growing number of people including Campbell believed that all could express their beliefs without the aid of a mediator, and that the diversity this created would advance unity. This provoked some interesting collaborative work within the people of faith – including a concept that blended the advancement of the mind and the soul.

Nobody really knows who thought of it at first. It seemed to be a collage of different conversations, viewpoints and considerations all coming together, but somehow it resulted in an outstanding piece of work. Contributors saw it as a living demonstration of their own creed, a tapestry of differing theology beautifully crafted into an evolving statement of faith that encouraged each one not to remain static in their own learning.

The idea was simple, yet profound in its mission. A weekly magazine was to be published every Saturday, so that families could read together on the Sabbath. Called *The Day of Rest*, this 'illustrated journal of Sunday reading' focused on investing in family life. It welcomed the diverse approaches that its contributors had to faith and education, and used songs, poems, hymns and prayers alongside articles about astronomy, ecology, Biblical narratives and serialised stories.

The team of writers was as varied as the topics. Richard Proctor, an English astronomer (1837-1888) used the drawings of the clergyman William Dawes to produce one of the earliest maps of Mars which brought him fame beyond his years, as well as a named crater. He was passionate about the wonders of the universe, and published books to stir the interest of the public.

Realising early on that his in-depth style was not digestible for the casual reader, he developed a more accessible form of writing, to communicate his knowledge in a way that captured the imagination. This successful approach was later copied by a 20th century television programme, *The Sky at Night*.

Hesba Stretton was the pen name of the writer Sarah Smith (1832–1911), best known for her children's literature. A fervent believer, she crafted stories to communicate values and godly principles for family life. Learning her trade through the editorial guidance of Charles Dickens, she developed a writing style that appealed to the masses but also challenged people about the social issues of poverty and education. Stretton was involved in the Religious Tract Society, an initiative to distribute evangelistic material to women, children and the poor.

Jean Ingelow (1820–1897) originally wrote for an evangelical youth publication, but soon developed into an acclaimed poet and author in her own right. Her poetry was praised within the literary world, and she even received recognition from the Poet Laureate, Alfred Tennyson. Even at the height of her success and material worth, she sought to distribute her royalties in the most socially considerate ways, often working in partnership with the local clergy to identify those most in need.

Dorothy Greenwell (1821-1882) was another poet motivated by faith values. Drawing on her religious heritage, she never shied away from challenging the reader with current issues. These included the slave trade, women's rights in education, gender status and the development of family life. Her complex character brought diversity to her work, as she exposed her audience to faith through stories that did not conform to any denominational grid.

Hugh Stowell Brown (1823-1886) was a preacher and social activist. Developing his own style of down-to-earth sermons, he focused on the poor and uneducated. Vast crowds came to his meetings and he challenged them about social ownership and care for one another. His activism extended to the establishment of localised banks that helped with money management and the distribution of financial support. He was also involved in peaceful conflict resolution.

Frances Verney (1819-1890) was the elder sister of the famous nurse and reformer, Florence Nightingale. A writer on many differing subjects, she used her position in society and the literary world to support reform of health and social care. With challenging practical examples she focused attention beyond the hospital, to sanitation and lifestyle choices.

George MacDonald (1824-1905) was a minister, poet and author, whose influence is still seen in books and films. His use of fantasy to communicate the theology of God's love was opposed by some traditionalists. Yet his tales were influential for other great authors. He mentored Rev. Charles Dodgson, whose penname was Lewis Carroll (author of 'Alice in Wonderland'), and their friendship helped to inspire the works we know and love today.

MacDonald's way of expressing the journey of faith through imaginary lands and mythical environments was a great inspiration to other writers, such as J.R.R. Tolkien and C.S. Lewis. Lewis even placed MacDonald as one of the characters in *The Great Divorce*.

These are just a few of the many contributors to the journal, an eclectic group. Their investment in this work took many forms, but they contributed to something that was more than just a weekly entertaining journal. Through their creative gifting, a much deeper message soaked into the land. It amplified a voice that was resounding already in society, an awakening of faith that appreciated diversity and learning. This was the story that was being read every Sunday, as families up and down the country gathered together. It was a call to all its readers to develop both the soul and the mind, subversively called *The Day of Rest*.

Thoughts

So many people walk around with a meaningless life. They seem half-asleep, even when they're busy doing things they think are important. This is because they're chasing the wrong things. The way you get meaning into your life is to devote yourself to loving others, devote yourself to your community around you, and devote yourself to creating something that gives you purpose and meaning.

(Mitch Albom: *Tuesdays with Morrie*)

Imagine a diamond being cut. At first glance, it seems unexceptional, its dirty, dull surface covered with a sticky deposit. Yet in the hands of a skilled craftsperson, something truly remarkable takes place.

Diamond cutting is complex, but two factors must be determined – the external and internal brilliance of the gemstone. Neither takes prominence over the other, as both are very significant. The process takes patience and a microscopic attentiveness to every detail and decision.

First the outside environment and the way the light radiates off each angle and intersection must be examined. Then the craftsman must consider what lies within, playing out every reflected beam in his mind. A cut too shallow or too deep, and its potential brilliance will be lost, never to be recaptured. The slightest defect will make a negative impact on its beauty.

The craftsman has a profound responsibility to respect the value of the gemstone and their own personal ability. Neither can express its true beauty without the other, yet when brought together, a synergy of exquisite elegance is displayed for all to see.

The collaborators on the journal, *Day of Rest*, appreciated each other's gift without an ideological viewpoint or political agenda. The respect for diversity propelled the work forward, as each contributor crafted not just their own story but the publication itself. This intriguing partnership leads my gaze towards the uncut diamond of our own stories, covered in the dirt of life yet of great worth.

Any attempt to fashion that stone ourselves results in a flawed and defective cut, as the ability to fully appreciate both the internal and exterior factors is outside of our own ability. It is strange to acknowledge such limitation, because our gifting enables us to cut perfectly the gemstones of others around. Yet the ability to shape ourselves is frustratingly just out of reach, so we need to place our life in the hands of fellow crafters.

It is such a vulnerable process to hand over the diamond that we cherish so deep within. Yet we all need the contribution of fellow lovers of Christ to shape our treasured hopes, dreams, and abilities that will shine His kingdom to those around. Such a partnership can only have been devised in the throne room of heaven, a characteristic of the master craftsman. It is a lesson self evident when we hold so precious the call of God upon our lives, a journey of collaboration that our own hands could never craft themselves.

Note 'D'
Activism

Introduction: To take a stand

The holy faith of our fathers has in many places been made a
form of entertainment ... That note of protest which began with
the New Testament and which was always heard loudest when the
Church was most powerful has been successfully silenced.

(A.W. Tozer: *Keys to the Deeper Life.*)

He was only forty-eight, but tuberculosis was slowly shutting his
body down, severely attacking his lungs and restricting his breath.
Friends were greatly concerned about his state of health, with fears
that if nothing was done, their dear colleague would soon depart this
mortal world. A plan was laid out that carried the hopes of restoration.
Money would be collected to fund temporary care and rest away from
the cold air of England, in the warmer climate of Portugal.

This was a precious demonstration of love from those his life
had impacted over the years. His genuine care for the wellbeing of
others had never been forgotten, and now when his body convulsed
in unbearable pain, friends came together and found a home for him in
the city of Lisbon. Yet he was greeted there with the same cold weather
as in his home nation, and before a month was out, the disease made
its fatal blow. On the 26th October 1751, Philip Doddridge took his
final breath, but his life lived on past that sorrowful day.

Doddridge was born in 1702, the twentieth child to parents who had seen eighteen of their children die in infancy. In this family, faith was more than just a set of rules. He never knew his grandparents, but their influence permeated the family line.

One of his grandfathers had stood up against what was later called the 'Clarendon Code' – legislation put in place to protect the established church after the Civil War and the restoration of the monarchy. Maintaining his beliefs that the enforced use of the *Book of Common Prayer* and the close ties to the king would clamp down upon religious freedom, he resigned his post as rector and became an unpaid non-conformist minister.

Doddridge's other grandfather was a Protestant minister who suffered persecution for his expression of faith. Steadfast in his commitment to not renounce his chosen path, he eventually fled from Prague to England. He set to work founding a grammar school in Kingston-upon-Thames with the belief that encouraging education goes hand in hand with the outworking of salvation in the individual and society.

Although they demonstrated their faith differently, they were unified in showing that beliefs of the heart require an outworking of practical decisions – acts of choice that may demand a high level of cost. They taught their children to pursue the convictions held deep within, and now they passed down this lesson to their grandchild, along with a copy of the treasured Lutheran Bible.

Doddridge's mother, Monica, moulded the early years of Doddridge's life. Although she died when he was only eight years old, this precious relationship of committed love and faithful learning continued to influence his life. He never forgot sitting by her side, while she taught him the stories of the Bible. She would use the pictorial tiles surrounding the fireside, interweaving each tale with historic examples of pilgrims who travelled committed paths of belief, including his grandparents.

Doddridge was to see the hand of death once again at the age of thirteen with the loss of his father, and when his guardian declared himself bankrupt, the family heirlooms were sold to save his custodian from the debtors' prison. Taking the only remaining family possession, his grandfather's Bible, he sought refuge at his sister's home, committed to pursuing a journey of following his Lord.

Even through these troubled and turbulent years, Doddridge excelled academically, and his abilities did not go unnoticed. He received an offer of educational support, but with a condition attached – at the conclusion of his studies he was to become a minister in the Church of England. Although it would have set this penniless man up for life, he felt called to the trail his grandparents had trod. He respected the Anglican faith, but knew he needed to challenge the apathy that had crept into church life. Rejecting the enticing offer, Doddridge set his sights on becoming a non-conformist minister, and through the help of a family friend and spiritual mentor he secured a place in a radical training college run by John Jennings.

Jennings was a strict and controversial tutor, mixing academia with ethic and moral studies. His purpose was to raise a band of preachers who would be able to stand against the tide of conformity and proactively demonstrate a life of social justice and faith. This was why his methods were tough, best described through the words of Doddridge himself:

> We preached this last half year, either home or abroad, as occasion required, and towards the beginning of it were examined by a committee of neighbouring ministers, to whom that office was assigned at a preceding general meeting. Mr. Jennings never admitted any into his academy till he had examined them as to their improvement in school learning, and capacity for entering on the course of studies which he proposed. He likewise insisted on satisfaction as to their moral character and the marks of a serious disposition (Bouge & Bennett, 1810).

This journey for Doddridge led him to eventually oversee a number of congregations and the development of a training college. Taking Jennings' example of challenging ayny form of apathy, he invested much of his time in highlighting an individual's personal responsibility. Aware that there was a growing educational divide in society, he wrote hymns that adapted eloquently written manuscripts into memorable statements, mindful that regardless of academic ability each person must encounter the power of the Gospel.

Writing such hymns as Oh Happy Day and *Now Let All* the Feeble Be Strong, Doddridge celebrated the joys of salvation while speaking out truth. He learned from his friend Isaac Watts, the prolific writer of such hymns as *Joy to the World*. Although their understanding of each other was sometimes as murky as the River Thames, their collaboration sparked moral and ethical reform around the country.

This was strengthened further by another friend, the famous revivalist preacher George Whitefield. Sharing pulpits and swapping sermon notes, both men entwined their faith with the issues of the day. It brought Doddridge great joy to witness Whitefield and his band of travelling preachers using outdoor sermons as a voice of protest, while promoting education and localised healthcare. This experiment was questioned on many fronts, but Doddridge held fast and won many of his doubters over by the sincerity of his cause.

Over the years Doddridge developed a network of relationships with friends and fellow travellers for revival. He hoped that by connecting various streams of action, it would spearhead a religious awakening, marrying an uncompromised preaching of God's Word with a commitment from believers to live out their faith in society. This passion drove him to write a book in 1745 called *The Rise and Progress of Religion in the Soul: Serious and practical addresses, suited to persons of every character and circumstance.*

In it he didn't pull any punches:

> When we view the conduct of the generality of people at home, in a nation whose obligations to God have been singular, almost beyond those of any other people under heaven, will any one presume today that religion has a universal reign among us? Will any one suppose that it prevails in every life; that it reigns in every heart? ...

> And where is the neighbourhood, where is the society, where is the happy family, consisting of any considerable number, in which, on a more exact examination, we find reason to say 'Religion fills even this little circle?' There is, perhaps, a freedom from any gross and scandalous immoralities, and external decency of behaviour, an attendance on the outward forms of worship in public, and, here and there, on the family; yet amidst all this, there is nothing which looks like the genuine actings of the spiritual and divine life ...

> There is no appearance of love to God, no reverence of His presence, no desires of His favour as the highest good: there is no cordial belief of the Gospel of salvation; no eager solicitude to escape that condemnation which we have incurred by sin; no hearty concern to secure that eternal

life which Christ has purchased and secured for His people, and which He freely promises to all who will receive him . . .

To a heart that firmly believes the Gospel, and views persons and things in the light of eternity, this is one of the most mournful considerations in the world . . . (Doddridge, 2011).

Less than six years later he died, without seeing everything he had hoped for come to fruition. Yet his words lived on in a new generation of believers. Within the same century a young Member of Parliament read a book that changed his life. Entitled *The Rise and Progress of Religion in the Soul*, it propelled William Wilberforce to consider his own faith and purpose in the world.

His subsequent actions contributed to the Slavery Abolition Act of 1833. A reformer in other issues, he became part of a band of believers daring to stand against the flow of social and moral injustice.

A century later another man came across Doddridge's words, who would become known as the 'Prince of Preachers' and would take the Gospel message to the masses. His name was Charles Spurgeon, and in a thankful letter to his mother he refers to a book that forever remained with him.

You, my mother, have been the great means in God's hand of rendering me what I hope I am. Your kind, warning Sabbath-evening addresses were too deeply settled upon my heart to be forgotten. You, by God's blessing prepared the way for the preached Word, and for that holy book, *The Rise and Progress (of Religion in the Soul)*. If I have any courage, if I feel prepared to follow my Saviour, not only into the water, but should He call me, even into the fire, I love you as the preacher to my heart of such courage, as my praying, watching mother (Drummond, 1992).

The life of Doddridge challenges us to look both at the beauty shining from creation as well as at the hidden abysses of evil. Our devotional path can both dance amid the fresh dew of a spring morning, as well as pace in a darkened, damp alleyway. We must mix faith-inspired hope with a clear focus on the pain of our world. While our heart leaps for joy at the words of our Father, we must also weep with those who weep and need his embrace. One without the other is alien to our faith.

Our loving God gave his only Son, and then Christ moulded our own hands and feet by that same unfathomable compassion. This unique commission requires us to be strong within our faith yet broken by a sacrificial love for others. The journey can be tough, but it is never lonely, because we are accompanied by those who have gone before us. People like Doddridge may not have agreed with every bit of our theology, yet what counts the most is that followers of Christ can stand firm in belief but be moved by compassion.

Quaker capitalism

We're passengers aboard the train, silent little lambs
amidst the pain. That's no longer good enough. And when
it's time to speak our faith, we use a language no one can
explain. That's no longer good enough.

And God knows it's a shame, because if we look to pass the flame,
we are not the worthy bearers of his name. For the world to know
the truth, there can be no greater proof, than to live the life.

(Brent Bourgeois and Michael W. Smith: *To Live the Life*)

It wasn't the easiest of moves, as it was surrounded by opposition, misunderstanding and financial challenges. This piece of land purchased on the 18th June 1878 held so much potential, but early work was hampered by bad weather and unforeseen struggles. By the time the first brick was laid in January 1879, the clay ground had become a sea of mud, with horses and carts struggling to transport materials to the building plots.

Some mocked because of these setbacks, gloating that this grand plan would not be finished on time. But sheer commitment, long hours and obsessive belief in the cause, led to the moment in 1880 when two brothers stood in front of their first finished cottages. It was a monumental step for the confectioners Richard and George Cadbury. These were more than just a few buildings; this was a sign that the family dream could one day be realised.

A couple of months earlier, the brothers had moved some of their cocoa business operations into the newly constructed warehouses next to the cottages. The carefully detailed blueprints brought amazement to staff: the buildings were not only well lit, but designed to stay cool in the summer and warm in the winter months. Each section was connected by tramways, which prevented heavy lifting and cumbersome travelling.

Whatever joys of a healthy working environment lay inside, they could not compare to what was designed for the staff and families outdoors. There was a large, spacious garden set aside for women, an orchard and natural areas, and gender specific swimming areas. As well as spacious affordable housing that were individually designed instead of crammed uniform buildings.

It was just the start. This experiment in alternative working conditions and living standards called Bournville would become a model village, a space where according to the New York Cosmopolitan reporter Annie Diggs:

> the very streets . . . laugh in the face of crude conventionalism. The monotony of capitalistic housing with rows of all-alike houses is prohibited. Why, it is the very joy of life among the villagers.
>
> The men not being overworked in the factory go straight to their gardens with keen delight . . . spade and barrow to work their allotments after factory hours. Charming woodlands haunts, fine pavilion for entertainments, cricket fields, football grounds, fishing pools and swimming places . . . reading rooms with the best books, literary societies, debating clubs and institutions for serious study (Cadbury, 2010).

This account was one of the articles that influenced the American chocolatier Milton Hershey to tour the premises, and consider his own social investment back in his country.

This living model village would also influence governmental initiatives called 'Garden Cities.' This was a bold idea to try and solve the problems of inner city life, with practical investment in living standards, spacious grounds and the fairer distribution of land. The initiative was spearheaded by Ebenezer Howard, who believed that the unjust nature of wealth and corporate land ownership resulted in many of the social evils of the day. If areas of the country were given back to individuals, he suggested it would create a sense of personal ownership that could echo the staggering results of Bournville, which yielded more produce than many farmed regions.

Other pioneering thinkers, including the confectioners Joseph Rowntree and the Fry family, shared this viewpoint and dared to question the social impact of common business practices. It was about a person's whole being. George Cadbury used to say 'We must not house our workers in a vile environment and expect their lives to be clean and blameless. We must do justice in the land.' He observed, 'Machinery creates wealth but destroys men,' and that placed the responsibility back into the hands of everyone around.

The ripple effect of their actions is still felt: these leaders in industry pioneered pension plans, housing and community sporting trusts. New systems were introduced, such as sick clubs so that workers who fell ill still had a stream of income to rely on, an increase in women's pay, and free transport for workers. In a time of intense industrial growth they boldly instituted half days on Saturday and a day off for bank holidays. It was missionary work worked out in ethical business, with lasting effects on modern working practices. But does that tell the whole story?

That moment when the two brothers stood outside their first constructed cottage was more than just the fulfilment of a personal dream. The hopes of previous generations were embedded in the bricks and mortar. These were dreams that found root two hundred years earlier in a revolutionary society of friends, commonly known as the Quakers.

This controversial group of pilgrims experienced the harsh hand of the law and state when they first declared their message of equality for all, in the early years of the 17th century. But as the decades passed, they grew not just in numbers but connections as well as they used their monthly, quarterly and yearly meetings to share news, discuss issues and support new ventures.

By 1689 a law had been passed that protected the Friends from persecution, but they were still not fully accepted in society. Therefore they had to be creative in business and finance. At a time when there were no national newspapers, their powerful network of relationships enabled them to effectively take hold of the new opportunities emerging from the Industrial Revolution.

By the 18th century, various Quaker families were instrumental in the development of the iron industry. As the 19th century dawned, they were leading the expansion of the railways, in not just the construction but also with the materials that were needed. On 27th September 1825, the world's first passenger train set off on a twelve-mile track, suitably named the 'Quaker Line.'

In Plymouth, William Cookworthy produced a new way of making fine china. In Staffordshire, Josiah Wedgwood established a new pottery business. James Clark developed shoes; Joseph Crosfields started a soap business that would eventually evolve into Lever Brothers, Unilever. During a time when banking was limited, Quakers provided services for the local communities. Praised for their honesty, diligence and skill in bookkeeping, these eventually developed into 74 Quaker banks including Barclays and Lloyds.

These pioneering works had faith principles running through every aspect of their operations which were founded in the original 'Advices'. These were guidelines of living shaped by the conversations taking place within Quaker gatherings. Collated in the *Christian and Brotherly Advices of 1738*, they covered all elements of daily life, including trading:

> That none launch forth into trading and worldly business beyond what they can manage honourably and with reputation among the Sons of Men, so that they may keep their words with all Men . . . It is advised that all Friends that are entering into trade and have not stock of their own to answer the trade they aim at be vary cautious of running themselves into debt without advising with some of their ancient and experienced Friends . . . nor to break promises, contracts and agreements in the buying and selling or in any other lawful affairs . . .

This commitment to one another, and the avoidance of the 'most pernicious practice' of paper credit, led to a further expansion of these *Advices* in 1833. One addition began: 'Dear Friends, who are favoured with outward prosperity, when riches increase not to set your hearts upon them'.

This code of practice influenced the father of Richard and George Cadbury. John Cadbury's rise in business was coupled by his involvement in the betterment of society. Concerned about child labour even before it was raised to public awareness by Charles Dickens' *Oliver Twist*, he was determined to reform the slave conditions of workhouses and chimney sweeps. Although he failed to convince many about a new machine that could clean chimneys, his continual campaigning and pursuit for justice eventually led to the banning of the use of 'climbing boys'.

His roles expanded further. Sitting on the committee for the 'Overseer of the Poor', he helped reform the working conditions on the factory floor. Involvement in the 'Steam Engine Committee' led to tackling the level of smoke and smog hanging in the city. Chairmanship of the 'Markets and Fairs Committee' dealt with unwholesome meats and fraudulent trading taking place within the slum areas. And work with his wife to tackle the levels of alcohol being consumed, soon developed into a project that his sons would carry forward: the development of an affordable cocoa drink that would provide a nutritious alternative to alcohol, 'hot chocolate'.

John Cadbury believed that faith was to be expressed in all aspects of life, every deed of value to the cause of salvation. The dream of justice and social reform that the brothers saw fulfilled that day in

1880 was only just a chapter of a wider story being outplayed. It was a narrative that their family had engaged with at the very beginning, when a group of misfits dared to declare that the Christian duty was not just about oneself.

The code they developed was fluid and allowed freedom of expression. One of those demonstrations was the missionary work and community service expressed by just business practice. Those early figures maintained a balance between financial growth and showing responsibility for the world they lived in that was to be nicknamed 'Quaker Capitalism'. This way of living involved all aspects of life, not just a pay-cheque or return in a shareholder's pocket.

Thoughts

> There is certainly untold pleasure in having to contend with overwhelming difficulties, and I sometimes pity those who have never had to go through it.
>
> (George Cadbury: *Chocolate Wars*)

Sometimes a page remains blank before a writer for many days, not because a particular story lacks excitement, but paradoxically, due to the great value of the narrative. The consideration of each line eats into time, while the author is acutely aware that because of his limitations, the task can never be completely fulfilled.

This was true for me when considering the Quakers' devotion to the Gospel message. For the Cadbury family, the simple dream that every life should be valued was an expression of divine worship. This was not designed to bring attention to some charismatic figure, but a prayerful statement that came from bended knees and dirt-filled hands.

I have wondered why this story captures me so much, and reduces my lexicon to a stumbling display of misplaced words. The answer, I believe, is found in the stories hidden from public gaze yet still able to be discovered and appreciated.

Imagine viewing a beautiful landscape. Hilltops and mountain ranges display grandeur of the highest order, vast crystal lakes and radiant green trees capture our gaze. It's a sight that could forever retain our focus. But what happens if we stare at the ground – the blades of grass or daisies that are readily trodden on? Simple as they are, there is an open invitation to every one of us to examine the three thousand species of grass or scrutinise the stunning florets within the makeup of the daisy.

This display of nature reveals a hidden complexity that can be so easily missed. They are all part of the landscape, each making a contribution to the sight before our eyes. Yet if one's gaze is centred on just the prominent and bold displays, it's easy to underestimate the glory that is hidden in the detail.

Take for example how George Cadbury regularly helped a movement called the Adult School. This was an initiative that helped provide basic education for adults who were living in the slums and struggled with learning. During this time, he came across an elderly man by the name of William White who had faithfully taught there every week, braving all kinds of weather to ensure he would never miss a class. It was a journey that White continued until his death at the age of 80.

Then there was a lady called Emma Wilson, a widow with seven children, who struggled to earn enough money to take care of her family. Having been exposed to the underbelly of child poverty, over time she began to help Richard Cadbury in setting up a crèche for poor or abandoned children. Despite being a single parent in a society where income was determined based on your gender, she rose to the challenge of helping those in need. Her sacrificial demonstration of love provided a welcome embrace for those who were yearning to be held safely within a parent's arm.

This is the landscape before us, and the reason why no writer can fully articulate its wealth and beauty. Many pilgrims' stories are simple, yet far too complex to put on a page. The fragrance of their life hangs sweetly in the air; their devotional footprint sinks deep into the soil. I believe that's the story of Quaker capitalism, and any works done in faith: a declaration of the worth of human beings and the value of living out Christ's love to make a difference in the world.

The outdoors

The eighteenth century . . . was a time when rioting, apparently
beyond the power of the law to control, was endemic . . .
The records of these uprisings reveal that they were most
frequent where Methodism was most active.

(Bernard Semmel: *The Methodist Revolution*)

A small, cross-eyed man made his way towards Kingswood. The year
was 1739 and George Whitefield knew this moment was significant.
His theatrical sermon style and tendency to challenge apathy meant
that he had been rejected from many pulpits, even from some church
buildings. Initial amusement had now turned to deep soul-searching.
He was convinced of his call to preach, but he questioned how he was
delivering his message.

As the days turned into months with preaching opportunities
closed to him, Whitefield had set his sights on a small coal-mining
village near Bristol. This experiment would not only be a pivotal point
in his own life, but bring about a movement that would shake the
United Kingdom and beyond.

As the name suggests, Kingswood was a wooded area that was
originally part of the king's estate. With the execution of Charles I in
1649, this piece of 'common land' was suddenly available for anyone
who would stake a claim. The land was in a prime location, rich with
timber and coal. Anyone who could construct a habitable home within
one day before dusk could set up a little mining operation with impunity
for squatting.

It was a fragile partnership where certain self-appointed lords of
the land earned a tithe from the increased activity, while the area was
being taken care of by the miners. As business grew, with the increased
industrial development and the rise in population, so did the demand
for profits. Men, women and children of all ages worked long hours
and in perilous conditions, just to meet the increased quota that was
being demanded.

In the 18th century, state-endorsed Toll Houses were introduced,
so workers who wanted to sell products not only had a levy from the
landowner, but now were charged just to leave home and return. In
addition, a number of factory workers had been shot dead by their
mill owner for protesting about the employment conditions. Tensions

rose, and the Kingswood miners had a history of protest. This close-knit community had demonstrated violently about food prices and the distribution of wealth. They were now rising up again against longer working hours and higher taxes, and walking towards their angry protest lines was a flamboyant little preacher who had never mined coal in his life.

At an early age, Whitefield had developed a passion for the dramatic, often skipping school so he could practice performances to make-believe crowds. Due to his poor background, he had to work his way through an Oxford education as a servant to other pupils. It was the lowest rank of student in a university world that saw status as everything. But tasks such as polishing shoes and writing assignments for his student masters never diminished his commitment to make something of his life.

A connection with a group of students that were seeking a new way of living out their faith started to shape this preacher-to-be. When his friends left for America, Whitefield took over the mantle of leader, and soon after preached his first public sermon, in Gloucester. It didn't take long before the theatrics that he was so fond of started to shine through, and people seemed to hang upon his every word.

Whitefield verbally painted living pictures of Biblical characters, dramatically moving from side to side, jumping, dancing and screaming, as he acted these scenes out to a captivated crowd. One of the most famous actors in Britain at the time commented enviously, 'I would give a hundred guineas if I could say "Oh" like Mr. Whitefield'.

In later years he would cross the seas to work with one of the founding fathers of the United States of America, Benjamin Franklin, contributing to a worldwide spiritual awakening and reform movement – but that day in 1739, he was looking towards a riotous coal mining community that God had put on his heart.

Whitefield first preached to two hundred people, and four days later, to two thousand people. The number then increased to five thousand and by the following Sunday, his journal records,

> At four I hastened to Kingswood. At a moderate computation there were about ten thousand people . . . All was hush when I began, the sun shone bright, and God enabled me to preach for an hour with great power, and so loudly that all, I was told, could hear me (Pollock, 1973).

In the weeks that followed, Whitefield continued to preach sermons that supported the miners' pursuit of justice, but encouraged them towards peaceful protests and dialogue between conflicting parties. He even prompted practical actions such as collecting money to build a school for their children, helping them to provide opportunities for the next generation.

As for Whitefield's first experiment in outdoor preaching, it was a marvellous success. He was not surprised, because he had been following the results of a couple of Welsh preachers, Howell Harris and Griffith Jones, who were daring to preach the Gospel on a hilltop, street corner, and any other accessible location. This new approach meant that they engaged with the community in new ways, facing local social concerns with practical demonstrations of the Gospel. The effects started to creep into lifestyle choices.

This lesson of blending the good news with the relevant issues of the day pointed Whitefield down the route of outdoor preaching. Observing how sermons could promote reform through the salvation call, led to him calling upon his friend, John Wesley, to help out. He needed someone to oversee this work as he left for America. At first Wesley 'could scarce reconcile myself . . . to this strange way of preaching in the fields'. Yet as history recounts, he soon followed the example of those Welsh preachers and that of his friend, and contributed to a movement that took open-air preaching to a whole new level.

Wesley's first hand experience of preaching where people lived and worked, helped him adapt his message to address the issues of the day. Kingswood demonstrated to him how a community could be changed, through challenging not just an individual's spiritual state, but also their responsibility to one another. This level of activism brought social and political change that some historians would argue as being the real revolution of Europe instead of France. As for Wesley's thoughts about this new experiment, you can find them in his journal:

> Kingswood does not now, as a year ago, resound with cursing and blasphemy, it is no more filled with drunkenness and uncleanness . . . wars and fighting . . . Peace and love are there (Wesley, 1872).

Thoughts

> They have trifled with the most holy, truthful, sincere,
> fervent feelings of people; they have bartered it all,
> all for money, for base earthly power.
>
> (Fyodor Mikhaylovich Dostoyevsky: *The Idiot*)

Dostoyevsky used the character of Prince Myshkin to express his views about a certain denomination. Yet the passionate cry of the man who examines the world around him and then responds to the prayer *'Your Kingdom come on earth'*, challenges any reader about their own expression of faith. And our band of travelling preachers a hundred years earlier, like Prince Myshkin, not only observed their world, but also considered their own personal response.

The city of Bristol was in the midst of change in the 18th century. Its population had trebled in size, becoming England's second largest city, as it enjoyed wealth from the immoral slave trade. Merchants found a new level of status, as the government favoured increasing this prosperous business. It was a land of possibility for entrepreneurs who could seize the moment and find the right idea to bring in the cash.

But these opportunities came with a heavy price tag. Not only was there an increasing black market of crime and extortion, but oppressive taxes and levies. In decades past, a craftsman was his own boss, providing food and income for their family. Now landowners and corporations were determined to take their cut for the sake of increased wealth. The chisel of greed crafted a new idol of individual gain.

Some commentators have called the Methodist movement a Methodist revolution, seeing the 'role of Methodism as a vehicle for its spiritual version of a democratic revolution'. A focus on organised protest, diversion of finances towards education and community development, and clearly articulated arguments meant that, 'this explosion of the energies of the masses was accompanied by a minimum of physical violence and bloodshed' (Semmel, 1974).

England wasn't saved from a revolution spreading across Europe; instead it pursued a stronger and more holistic one. The reforms in some countries were pursued through violence and self-interest, but these travelling Methodist preachers pointed to goals which centred on the betterment of society and not just their own position.

They promoted the building of schools and the expansion of clubs that took care of those who were sick and in need of help. In the simplicity of their outdoor preaching, they radically engaged with the pain, need and hope of society. Without using it as a political platform or grandstanding event, those preachers simply went where they were most needed. They declared in both word and deed, that giving out a cup of water to those who are thirsty is a proactive demonstration of compassion.

A story within a story

I am more than ever convinced that the half will never be told.

(Rev. Elvet Lewis: *The Awakening in Wales* –
his firsthand observations of revival)

James Naylor gingerly took hold of his quill, his hand shaking as it moved slowly towards the parchment. It was only a matter of time before his frail body took its final breath. Whatever had spurred him in the past to declare the passions he held so deep within his soul, the ticking of the clock became his final motivation, spurring him to craft these words that would remain long after he departed this world.

A few years earlier in 1656, he had undergone the most brutal of punishments. Forced to walk through London while being flogged, he was then brought to a platform to have his tongue bored through with a hot iron and the letter '*B*' branded on his forehead. It was a public statement to all that he was a blasphemer of both God and state. Yet this was only the first part of a long, drawn-out process aimed to break his spirit. Exposed to public ridicule and violence at the pillory, and then made to walk the streets of Bristol for another series of floggings and public humiliation, he never recovered from this prolonged act of vengeance.

Although what he stood for was not to everyone's liking, the barbaric nature of this determined judgment shocked many onlookers and even some of his accusers. His crime was to ride into Bristol in 1656 on a donkey, while people laid garments down before him on a rain soaked path. The symbolism of women singing 'Holy, Holy, Holy is the Lord God of Israel', gave government and church authorities the opportunity to put the movement he was a part of in the dock. More importantly, they used the 'blasphemer' as a vivid example of what they could do to those who challenged their power.

This accusation of 'messianic heresy' wasn't new, for there had been others who had proclaimed they were either Christ himself or the 'Spouse of Christ'. Those accused had been handed to the local magistrate and briefly imprisoned. So the savage sentence for a man who didn't publicly declare divinity but stirred controversy with his entrance, sickened many citizens. Some even questioned why the case was being determined by Parliament itself instead of the local courts.

Petitions and letters were raised, urging Oliver Cromwell to support this religious group which had helped him come to power. Yet while he queried the power of Parliament in a letter that was cheekily dated Christmas Day, his need for Westminster's support for his own political goal of a new form of monarchy, meant that he eventually sided with the 'House'.

For the authorities, Naylor was more than just a man; he symbolised a threat to order. The religious movement he was part of needed to be stopped before it ripped through the fabric of the nation. It had played an integral part in the English Revolution, as a voice for the people on equality, distribution of wealth and land ownership.

Now it was fostering a growing resentment against the inactiveness of the new government and their failed promises of freedom. What better way to try and muzzle that dangerous voice than to focus on the donkey-riding preacher and the movement he represented, Quakerism? The sentence was passed in 1656, and Naylor accepted his punishment with the statement, 'God has given me a body; He will, I hope, give me a spirit to endure it'.

Three years later, he looked at his parchment. In just a few short months he would be dead at the age of 43. Many had turned their backs on him since that ill-chosen decision at Bristol, and few of the '*Friends*' that he held dear turned up for his show trial. Although in great pain, while he still had life, he was not going to remain silent.

The bold words that once shook the corridors of power were now replaced with broken words from a broken man. His simple hope was that its display of holy vulnerability would rally pilgrims of faith to continue to fight the cause, without making the same mistakes he had made.

The words he wrote would be known as his confession, a humble account of his weakness, strength and determination to love his Lord. He laid bare how he had heard his God speak while ploughing a field, and learned to pursue the 'Inner Light' of the Spirit within. Stepping out in unquestioning obedience that sometimes meant deep cost, he had a passion to lay hold of the dream of seeing God's kingdom come on earth. His determination captivated many hearts, stirring people to critique their own faith and that of their nation.

Each sentence opened up more of his life, humbly acknowledging how the growing crowds of admiring followers began to affect his opinion of himself. How he

> exalted in himself, because of the gifts, and glory in his strength and wisdom, and so grow wanton against the Life, from whence he has it; and so through feeding on the gifts, ceases to walk humbly with the Giver in his own vessel.

> Here man forgets his God, and so withers at the root, and
> be the tree never so great it will fall in the end, 'and great
> will be the fall thereof' (Sewel, 2010).

Prostrate before the cross of his Saviour, Naylor's deep regret radiated through his words. He recounted his ride into Bristol, how although he begged the women to stop their praise, he knew inwardly that his protests were weakened by self-adulation. He painfully recalled how Hannah Stranger had addressed him as the 'only begotten Son of God', and her husband said, 'thy name shall be no more James Naylor but Jesus'. His conviction about the 'Inner Light', that the priestly role was superseded by the equality of all believers, had led him to passively accept what others expressed as the voice of God.

It was a painful admission about the freedom of thought that the Quaker and Ranter position had declared. Naylor pointed out that this powerful, government-shaking message that all could hear from God, must be subject to the discipline of the Spirit. His conclusion was that personal freedom required submission to one another. Critiquing earthly constructs such as Parliament and the established Church cannot exempt us from removing the plank in our own eye.

Naylor died in 1660, after being found lying in a field by Huntingdon – whether he had stumbled due to illness or had been robbed was unclear. He was brought to a *Friend's* house in Kings Rippon where he took his final breath. His closing words reflected a man who knew his own mistakes, yet found great peace in something far beyond earthly understanding.

> There is a Spirit which I feel, that delights to do no evil, nor
> to revenge any wrong, but delights to endure all things, in
> hope to enjoy its own in the end. Its hope is to outlive all
> wrath and contention, and to weary out all exaltation and
> cruelty, or whatever is of a nature contrary to itself. It sees
> to the end of all temptations, as it bears no evil in itself,
> so it conceived none in thought to any other. If it be
> betrayed it bears it; for its ground and spring is the mercies
> and forgiveness of God . . . (ibid, 2010).

Thoughts

> Whoever controls the past controls the future, and
> whoever controls the present controls the past.
>
> (George Orwell: *1984*)

The life of James Naylor was truly a controversial one. He passionately pursued heavenly justice, and never wanted to preach anything that had first not lived deep inside his heart. His sermons of 1653 shocked the nation with their directness. Their blend of salvation and activism rallied people to both personal repentance and sacrificial acts of compassion.

In the space of a few short years, Naylor had become a central figure in the English Revolution. Yet his fleshly weaknesses brought his morality and conduct into question, and he was described as:

> a gifted, sensitive man, overtaxed, living on his nerves, short of food, owing to fasting, and shorter still of sleep, and fatally attractive to hysterical people, especially to hysterical women (Hill, 1972).

Naylor lived in an exciting and disruptive time of conflicting agendas. From self-appointed messiah figures to anarchic activist groups, the noise of differing worldviews echoed throughout the revolutionary land. But no matter how loudly opinions were amplified, a distinctive voice started to be heard that came from a band of religious rebels, later known as the Quakers.

These 'Roundheaded Rogues' raised a chorus of growing conviction that their actions would usher in God's Kingdom on earth. They declared a message that challenged the highest seats of earthly power in government and business: that knees must bow to something far greater. Mixing spirituality with social justice, their prophecies, sermons and prayers were accompanied by demands for fair distribution of land and pay.

Rejecting status or mediation, they considered all persons equal and equipped to hear and declare the voice of their Creator. All could prophesy, all could pray for the sick, and all could preach the Gospel. It was a dangerous message in a church-state, which explains why the established powers wanted to determine Naylor's punishment instead of leaving it to a local courtroom.

In this narrative is a lesson that we can all learn. The famous journal of George Fox (seen as the founder of Quakerism) described the author's central role while sidelining much of Naylor's controversial participation. The trouble at Bristol was only part of the growing tensions within this diverse grouping of people. With the pressure on them since the restoration of the crown to protect themselves from a revengeful monarch, some decided that more control and discipline were required.

Fox ceased collecting evidence of miracles happening throughout the network, and the messianic hope of bringing in God's Kingdom was replaced with pacifism and non-participation in certain roles. As a 17th century Royalist poet described, 'The Quaker who before did rant and roar. Great thrift now will tell ye on'. This rag-tag, wild movement slowly developed into a national organisation that needed to communicate an acceptable message to the masses validating its journey.

George Orwell's observation about controlling the past seems insightful. By 1694, the Quakers were known as Fox's movement, yet in the 1650s some even suggested that if there ever were a head it would be Naylor. In a debate in the House of Commons in 1656, Colonel Cooper remarked that 'He (Naylor) writes all their books . . . Cut off this fellow and you will destroy the sect' (ibid, 1972). His point about authorship of their pamphlets was factually incorrect, but it highlighted the slippery nature of this revolutionary group of people.

I admire both the characters of Fox and Naylor; their examples of faith challenge my own sense of apathy. Yet we must learn the lessons of their frailty. The stories we tell lose a beautiful edge when we trim out the parts we feel ashamed of or disappointed in. As we sow compassion into the world, there will be days of success as well as painful reminders of our mistakes. Yet if we humbly accept that our whole life carries a story beyond earthly sight, grace shines forth. And it is this unearned grace of redemption that outshines the cleverest spin we may add to our own wonderful narrative.

Note 'E'
Obedience

Introduction: the attitude of the heart

Faith is deliberate confidence in the character of God
whose ways you may not understand at the time.

(Oswald Chambers: *My Utmost for His Highest*)

Scripture is infused with raw tales of devotion in the lives of pilgrims of the faith. While none surpass that of our precious Lord and Saviour, many human stories exemplify the unfathomable depths of obedience and faith, encouraging each fellow traveller in their own path of piety.

In one such narrative, a man faces a decision where status, outside opinions and the question of character are all factors in a pre-destined path. The unfolding story followed the decision-making process as he deals with his world being turned upside down. Plans for the future are shipwrecked on the rocks of recent news, with the jagged edge of doubt causing painful internal debate. Finally he finds a course of action to protect his loved one and his own moral standing.

Joseph's conclusion was to quietly separate from his betrothed, as she was carrying a child that was not his own. He settled on this compassionate compromise not to publicly humiliate her, until he was challenged by a dream. It was a word sent from God, that the unborn child was part of an intricate divine plan that would lead his people to deliverance and the forgiveness of sins.

The story of Jesus' earthly father is well known from the nativity tales told every year. But when an angel appears to the man who is questioning the moral standing of his wife to be, it's a moment that captures the rawness of life. Joseph had heard the news from the woman pledged to him that she now carried a child. The story he heard seemed unbelievable, and the logical question was, 'If this is not my child, who is the father?'

I cannot imagine the tension Joseph must have internally battled with. His plan to try to rectify it quietly seems to convey a war between his love of Mary and his commitment to ethics. Yet he received a message from God to accept the child, and he cradled the baby as his own, believing that the conception was a divine moment involving no other human party. It was a tall order, but as Rembrandt depicted in his painting *Joseph's Dream*, obedience was displayed through the vivid colours of devotion.

The word obedience covers many different interpretations and emotions: maybe a child's response to their parent's word, or an office worker complying with the order of their manager. It could be obeying the highway code or state law. Its definition encompasses respect, honour and maybe even the fear of failure to comply.

I have always associated the prayer, *'Your kingdom come, Your will be done, on earth as it is in heaven'*, with the outworking of revival. Touching the wondrous texture of such a divine moment is linked to living out the Saviour's prayer. Scripture is full of references to the kingdom, to be sought after like a treasure in a field or a fine pearl purchased by a merchant. But the root of my own motivation for seeking such a pearl is challenged when I consider Matthew 25.

Here we see God's kingdom represented in three distinct images: the waiting bridegrooms, the talents, and the sheep and goats. The series of parables is clear about the participants' responsibility. First, the bridegrooms had to make sure their marriage lamps were full of oil to be lit. Second, the talents had to be used wisely, and third, the least of Christ's brethren had to be cared for. While there are great rewards of such responsibility, the sober implications of failure are inescapable: missing the wedding, having talents taken away, and the goats being separated from the sheep.

These implications became a hidden motivation for the outworking of my faith. I needed to make sure I was always ready for my Lord, that my talents were used correctly and that I demonstrated my love to those around. I made an impressive show of Christian service as I pursued the revival message. But was I just a modern day Pharisee, who followed the rules yet never grasped the heartbeat within?

The root meaning of obedience is focused on the heart attitude of the one who hears. It is firmly embedded in a relational context beyond just lip-service. When obedience is within the framework of our faith, it represents more than a set of rules and actions.

History gives many suggestions about how to bring about revival. The Welsh revivalist Evan Roberts gave four keys: confess all known sin, search out all secret and doubtful things, confess the Lord Jesus openly, and pledge to fully obey the Spirit. Finney had his principles of revival and Wesley provided methodical rules of practical living. It may be tempting to think that revival will follow automatically. Yet in their original setting, these statements of promised revival were less a blueprint than a prompt to consider one's own heart.

These famous texts did not come from the starting point of revival, but were birthed in an intense realisation of faith. They vary from a strict and sometimes unhelpful code that Wesley tried to observe, to Roberts' fluid reliance upon the Holy Spirit that could be used to avoid taking a stand on pressing issues. Yet in all their human imperfections, these people were alive with the energy of devotion to their Saviour. This underlying motive formed their steps and decision-making processes more than the headline principles they later shared with those who sought revival.

It was a challenge in their day, and it is a challenge to us now. In our present world we expect immediate answers to our questions. By seeking words of wisdom from the podium, framing them into handy bullet-points, then following them to the letter, will we see the results of our prayers and hopes? Although it may be good to focus on such treasured wisdom, we must never loose sight of the roots of devotion and vague insights these statements were birthed within.

This leads us back to Joseph's story. At the crossroad of decision, where society's logic dictated a certain path, he chose another trail that revealed the beautiful gem of devotion. This precious jewel of trust was not just about his journey, but about Mary's willingness to follow God's call. Yes she was 'blessed' to be chosen, but she still needed to utter those words of obedience.

We have the benefit of hindsight to make sense of their decisions, but sometimes that reinforces our own insistence about knowing our future path in minute detail. Yet we seem to be invited to walk on a pilgrimage without a completed map, to be content with the simplicity of hearing God's Word even when we don't fully understand where that leads.

Obedience is a heart attitude expressed through sacrificial decisions, made without a template to follow. It leaves a captivating and lasting fragrance. The words of Mary as she journeyed into the unknown stand the test of time. *'I am the Lord's servant, may it be to me as you have said'*.

The daily cross

If you believe, you shall receive. For there is not a trouble or care
the good Lord can't relieve. Oh, he is just the same today. All you
have to do is trust and pray and believe. You must believe.

(Theme song to the *Allen Revival Hour* radio show)

The year is 1957 and under the glare of bright spotlights, a preacher
looks out on the crowd. This speaker was enjoying the heights of
success, with his evangelistic crusades being held in the biggest tent
of any ministry of the day. The new medium of television was being
used to film the services, bringing his message of faith and healing to
the American TV-dinner audience.

It was an exciting time, with miraculous demonstrations capturing
the attention of believers and sceptics alike. Doctors who were paid
by the media to verify what was being recorded, stood in disbelief
as bones reformed, sight was restored and limbs reappeared before
their eyes.

This evidence of God's power to the masses formed the early days
of Christian television. Some used this new form of communication
as a way of sparking debate about debt, justice, work ethics and
educational standards, but none tackled the controversial issue of race
equality as intensely as this preacher in his crusades.

The presence of a black worship leader to guide the congregation
and the television audience in song was not missed in a national
atmosphere when the civil rights issue was very much in sight. At a
time when Rosa Parks refused to give up her seat in a segregated bus,
and protests erupted about school integration, this preacher refused
to practice segregation in his meetings. This was a bold statement,
particularly during his tour of the South, a mix of miracles and
engagement in social justice.

This 'man of faith and power' was named Asa Alonso Allen. His
Miracle Magazine, a record of crusade events and testimonies, was
distributed to over five million people, and the 'Allen Revival Hour'
radio show was broadcast on one hundred and eighty-six stations
every single day. He was one of the stars of the 'Voice of Healing'
movement that was sweeping across the States and beyond, a number
of itinerant ministers who declared the Gospel message with signs and
wonders following.

Yet behind the remarkably successful ministries of such characters as Jack Coe, Oral Roberts and William Branham, lay a background story of infighting and accusations. Sadly, subtle rivalries over the type of healing and the size of attending crowds would cloud this most breathtaking of Christian movements.

These arguments were not just between preachers and their teams. Some local congregations formed themselves into committees, to control when and how the travelling preachers would operate within their towns. They aimed to protect their flocks, shape the sermon content and manage any controversial issues that these ministries might provoke.

But however well meaning these agendas were, the focus of these committees was also who had the final rights to secure converts and finances following the crusade. Various parties built theological fortresses and battle plans around the events. Allen had often experienced the joys and pains of working with such groups, but one moment would forever stand out. It was the infamous Knoxville, Tennessee incident in 1955 which would taint his reputation even after his death in 1970.

Driving back to his motel after an evening's service, he needed to pull over and take in some fresh air. As he stopped the car he found that the media, police and several local pastors were surrounding his vehicle. Allen was tested and ticketed for driving under the influence of alcohol. The following day the newspaper headlines read, 'Evangelist Allen arrested for drunk driving'.

Allen's colleague, Brother Rogers, who was also in the car, recounts his version of this notorious story. Due to the size of the crowds that were coming to Allen's meetings, they had chosen an auditorium to house the services instead of a local church property. The decision angered the local committee, as their cut of the collected tithes depended on the use of their own grounds. With this new meeting location, any collection would now be passed to the headquarters of the national denomination instead.

Allen and the committee refused to back down, and the departing words were accusations and threats, leaving an unstable foundation for the developing crusade meetings.

After one of the services, Allen stopped off at a local cafe for some food and drink. He had always practiced fasting before his healing crusades. After finishing a glass of milk he remarked that his drink tasted funny, 'perhaps it was blinky', meaning just about to go sour.

Soon after he started to drive again he felt slightly dizzy, so he pulled over and asked his friend to take the wheel instead. As they stopped the car, they found themselves surrounded. In front of local media and the pastors who had earlier disagreed with him over the income from the event, this healing evangelist was tested for alcohol in a Southern state.

Regardless of differing versions of the story, it was allegations of drunkenness that followed him to his death in 1970, in the Jack Tar hotel room, San Francisco. Found slumped in an easy chair, dead, rumours abounded that his room was covered with empty liquor bottles. Reactions in the faith community varied, but the majority believed the reports of death by alcohol.

Soon the stories of miracles and social engagement were replaced with condemnation and disgust, even to the point of eradicating footage of his previous crusades. It wasn't until 2007 that new evidence emerged that questioned the events and accusations. History showed that he was never the beast that his enemy made him out to be.

Allen's past and future were to merge in this moment on the light-drenched stage in 1957. The spectacular miracles happening at his meetings had become national talking points. *(Over his ministry years, doctors and the crowds verified dramatic events as they happened right before their eyes. These included a clinically obese woman who had been prayed for and left behind the remains of her excess fat on the floor. There was also the healing of a boy that had no bones in his legs until he was prayed for, and then could stand and run).* The audience that night was expectant that the same dramatic things would happen again.

As Allen continued to look across the crowd, he noticed what he termed the 'wanna-be preachers and partners': those who coveted the dramatics, the lights, and the cameras for their own work. It was here that he stopped, and took a breath. A hush fell upon the crowd, as he began to recount the hidden story that went past the glitzy glamour of public recognition. He began his story with two Scripture passages.

> If any man will come after Me, let him deny himself, and take up his cross daily,

> I beseech you, therefore, brethren, by the mercies of God, that ye present your bodies . . .

As he finished reading, his words struck deep into the heart of the audience,

Many of you are talking about supernatural things. Many of you are talking about the gifts of healing. Wonderful! Many of you are desiring the gift of miracles. Great! You're talking about signs and wonders, and strange and mighty things. Marvellous!

But I'm going to bring you down out of the sky tonight, and talk to you about a reasonable service. Don't get mad at me, now. It's all right to get up in the sky. But there's only one right way to get up there, and that's to get on the ladder and start climbing. And you can't start on the tenth rung first! You must start on the bottom rung. And that's old-fashioned holiness, giving your body to God, a living sacrifice, which is none other than your reasonable service (Allen, 1957).

The mood in the miracle tent suddenly changed, as he guided his listeners to the cross of obedience. He told the story of how he and his family had pursued the calling on their lives, paying the price as they did so:

We moved into a new area one time, and we didn't have a bit of milk for our baby nor a bit of money to buy milk … We couldn't afford to rent a house, so we stretched up a clothes line across the back of the [church] hall and hung up our sheets to make ourselves a room to live in.

He recounted the prayers and concerns about where the next dollar bill or food parcel would come from. From time to time stopping to point towards the congregation and say

You want to be a preacher, fine! But I'm going to try my best to talk you out of it tonight! And if I can, then God never called you in the beginning! If He has, it doesn't matter what I say, I can't talk you out of it! (ibid, 1957).

In the packed meeting hall he described the solitary nights in prayer where faith and loneliness seemed to walk hand in hand, and the times when he would look at his young family and feel ashamed that he was unable to provide the basic essentials. He recalled how he shed tears as he found extra hours in the day to work between meetings, just to be able to bring back a loaf of bread and milk for a crying child.

The stories went back to their lives as a young married couple, including their honeymoon when they had no money, but were committed to travelling the country to preach the Gospel message. Of the shame he felt when he saw his new wife going into the forest to cut firewood to sell, the meals of leftovers and scraps, and homes that were little more than sheds in a backyard next to a chicken coop.

Allen continued with his experiences of empty church meetings and unresponsive altar-calls along with sporadic answers to prayer. This rollercoaster ride of highs and lows was the sacrificial journey of obedience, something that seemed completely opposite to the public stage and miraculous signs that many of the audience were yearning for.

The evening was drawing to a close when Allen said,

> Just before I finish tonight, and make this altar call, I want to instruct every one of you about one more thing. There will be many times when you will be tempted to shun the small churches, and the small towns, hoping to accept meetings in the big churches. Be careful…Don't give place to the desire to be thought somebody big and important (ibid, 1957).

It was a lesson he lived out after every meeting, as the television lights faded and the final note was sung. Refusing to be guarded by his entourage and forsaking the comfort of the hotel room and hot shower, he committed to stay on in the tent long after the meeting had closed, listening, praying, crying and laughing with whoever was still there. This was all the more outstanding when you consider his meetings would last for many hours due to his determination to pray individually for as many sick people as he could.

The story he recounted that night would eventually be written in a book called *My Cross*, many copies of which shamefully ended up dumped, as the rumours of his death filtered into the gossip columns of church life.

Thoughts

> To obey is better than sacrifice. I want more than Sunday and Wednesday nights. Cause if you can't come to me every day, then don't bother coming at all.
>
> (Keith Green: *To Obey is Better than Sacrifice*)

The cross is not a pleasant symbol. It represents one of the most cruel and humiliating of deaths ever devised by humanity. As A.W. Tozer wrote,

> The cross of old Roman times knew no compromise; it never made concessions. It won all its arguments by killing its opponent and silencing him for good. It spared not Christ, but slew Him the same as the rest ... it always has its way. It wins by defeating its opponent and imposing its will upon him. It always dominates. It never compromises, never dickers nor confers, never surrenders a point for the sake of peace (Tozer, 2005).

This long drawn out execution was a display of imperialistic strength, parading a convicted criminal in humiliation for all to see. Some would be made to carry the heavy crossbar to its final destination. The rope and splinters buried deep into their flesh as the weight of the wood took its toll upon the body already weakened by beatings. Each step brought them closer to death.

If the condemned provoked hatred from the soldiers or their crime was considered severe, they would be attached to the cross with nails instead of rope. As the cross was lifted into place, the dying individual gasped for air, struggling for life. It was a long and humiliating punishment, where the naked body was left on show with no sense of dignity or privacy for bodily excretion.

Even when the soldiers quickened the process by breaking the legs, it was still agonising. The crucified were unable to pull their body up to relieve their chest muscles, slowly suffocating without the ability to relieve any of the pain.

Despite the unspeakable horror of this barbaric death journey, an intimate interaction is seen between our Saviour and his disciples. Long before he was to be arrested and taken to his death, he asked his friends, 'Who do you think I am?' When they responded, he ordered them to tell no one else. And as he explained what was to come, he said,

> *Whoever wants to be my disciple must deny themselves and take up their cross daily and follow me. For whoever wants to save their life will lose it, but whoever loses their life for me and for the gospel will save it (Mark 8: 34-35).*

It's hard to imagine what must have gone through the minds of his hearers. To add to the extreme personal cost, they had to be prepared to die for a cause that had to be kept secret. They had seen revolutionaries crucified, publicly declaring in their final breath why they were willing to lay their life down. Yet the disciples' sacrifice would have to be privately founded on a personal interaction with their Lord.

A.A. Allen was right to draw the attention of the crowd away from the glamour and glory of the public stage, and focus instead on the sober message of following Christ through embracing the cross daily. His message was echoed by Tozer as he challenged his readers that

> We must do something about the cross, and one of two things only we can do – flee it or die upon it ... the cross will cut into our lives where it hurts worst, sparing neither us nor our carefully cultivated reputations (ibid, 2005).

The embracement of the cross is done within the secret and hidden place of intimacy. Where its splinters cut deep into our flesh of human frailty, but the balm of his love soaks deep in a humble and contrite heart. This I believe is the challenge of obedience, one that is seen from the throne room of heaven and whose applause is heard within the secret realms of our worshipful heart.

The gauntlet of obedience

O for a thousand tongues to sing, my great Redeemer's praise,
the glories of my God and King, the triumphs of his grace.

My gracious Master and my God, assist me to proclaim, to
spread through all the earth abroad, the honours of thy name.

(Charles Wesley: *O for a Thousand Tongues*)

Three people came together to finalise a plan that seemed illogical
to any passing observer. With little money, no team except themselves
and minimal connections in the area, they had set their sights on
conducting an evangelistic tent crusade in Bootle, Liverpool. They
were to go into a location that had been hit hard in an unsettling
economic period, so there would be little chance of recovering the
expense of such an endeavour. Their message of hope would face a
critical reception from those experiencing the harsh reality of life.

It was not easy, but they knew God had led them. When asked
years later if they would do the same again, the leader of this brave
and sometimes crazy group of three simply replied, 'Oh yes.'

The year was 1934, and the team of three (Esaiah Davies, the song
leader and soloist, Horace Trembaith, the campaign organiser and
pianist, and Edward Jeffries, the preacher and healing evangelist)
knew that the atmosphere to launch their step of faith was anything
but stable.

Fearful insecurity had begun to take centre stage in Britain, from
political developments with Oswald Mosley, who formed the British
Union of Fascists and his 'black shirt' brigade, to disturbing reports of
how political protest was being violently clamped down by the
German authorities, culminating a few months later in the 'Night of
the Long Knives'. In the corridors of British power and the corner shops
of local communities, a dreadful trend was recognised. Political
instability in Europe and apprehension for the future was accentuated
by what many citizens were facing economically.

Britain was still struggling with the effects of an economic depression.
Budget cuts, wage reductions, mass unemployment and questions
about care for the poor, were all central topics. The country's finances
were struggling and heated debates had come to the forefront
with British economist John Maynard Keynes, who was developing
the theory of macroeconomics. His suggestion that a government

deficit should be welcomed to stimulate localised spending, stirred arguments from those who considered that balancing the budget was a wiser and more prudent approach.

It was a debate that rocked an already fragile ship. The government was facing an uncertain period of time. A collaboration called 'the National Government' had been formed in 1931 due to disagreement about cuts in the previous ruling Labour government. In what seemed a politically orchestrated move to increase the share of the Conservative party input while diminishing union influence, this new all-party collective was voted into government with unprecedented support.

Even though this party was led by Labour Prime Minister Ramsey McDonald, his own political manoeuvring had led to a majority Conservative cabinet that governed much of domestic policy. With little influence at home, McDonald concentrated on foreign policy, but continued to be troubled by the demise of his beloved Labour party. By the beginning of 1934 his leadership, even in its weakened state, was becoming a national concern. Incoherent speeches led to his mental stability being questioned, amid increasing disquiet over the political developments in Germany.

Unease with the government impacted everyday life, as riots, protests, concerns for employment and youth disengagement all affected 1930s Britain. Questions about homeland security and stability, and international developments made life ever more complex. Political debate was more than just words spoken from a podium; it now carried implications for the weekly pay check. Concerns about putting food on the table and having a job for life were raised in local activism which challenged who was really in charge of the country.

In this uncertain climate, three people decided to step out into the unknown. Their decision to start a crusade at the end of May 1934 resulted in a summer-long campaign that saw between seven to ten thousand people attending a three-thousand capacity tent every night. Response to the salvation call danced hand in hand with the flow of miracles taking place. A previously sceptical minister commented,

> First of all men's lives are being changed, homes are different, children are better cared for, debts are being paid, and thousands of dear people have a song in their hearts. Melody is seen and heard where once discord ruled. This is the greatest miracle and is brought about by the direct intervention of God through our Lord Jesus Christ in the affairs of men and women. Where spiritual

blindness rules, the eyes of the soul have been opened. The chains of sin have been broken and there is great joy in the city (Green, 2010).

The meetings filtered into home and work life, as the topic of the crusade replaced the uncertain political issues of the day. Tales of miracles took prominence at the dining room table, on public transport, in social houses and business premises. It wasn't because of a well-organised event or fancy stage presentation; instead it was simply,

God did what no amount of organising and advertising, canvassing and counselling could ever do. Materially the campaign was launched on a shoestring but when the heavens are rent, the mountains flow and God comes down and no more is needed (ibid, 2010).

People reported a sweet aroma when they entered the canvas tent that complimented the sound of collective singing that rose up in the worship service. Regularly there would be shouts of joy as someone leapt out of a wheelchair or saw the faces of the crowd for the first time from their once-blind eyes. These phenomena defied rational explanation. Jefferies knew it wasn't down to him, so he went off on holiday, leaving the crusade to continue in all its supernatural power.

As the tent finally came down at the end of the summer season, the meetings continued in various church halls and cinemas. A decision was made to construct a wooden chapel on the site where the tent once stood, and on New Year's Day in 1935, Bootle Bethel was opened with the nickname 'the Wooden Cathedral'. Just as in the tent, no matter what its capacity, there was never enough space for the crowds. They were a diverse group, all finding Gospel assurance in a time of national uncertainty.

Edward's father Stephen and Uncle George had already touched communities with a series of evangelistic healing crusades. While travelling together, with Stephen as the preacher and George as the music director, they discovered an anointing to pray for the sick. With different personalities, one exuberant and the other solemn, they both had the fortitude to face the hardest of challenges. Whether it was Stephen who would jump off the stage during the middle of a sermon to heal a sick member of the congregation, or George who preached the Gospel in the Royal Albert Hall with eyes of fire, these two brothers were making a mark on the history of faith.

Their transforming encounter with the Lord during the Welsh Revival of the early 20th century catapulted them both into a radical pursuit of God's mission. George became the more popular of the two brothers, helped by his organisational abilities and people-management skills, while Stephen preferred to keep things as simple as possible, but insisted on being hands-on with every aspect of the ministry. This led them on differing paths, with both facing opposition and struggle in the work they had established over the years.

Stephen came under more personal scrutiny from the press, particularly about his wealth and image. He replaced his plain clothes with a priestly outfit and sometimes seemed to receive the adulation of others instead of directing it elsewhere.

George, who had successfully developed the Elim movement, now faced disagreements about the direction he was leading the work in. This led to him leaving his organisation and setting up the 'Bible Pattern Church Fellowship'. It was not the easiest of splits, but it did bring the two brothers together again in the early 1940s, to work alongside Edward.

Stephen died a few years later from what he described as letting 'this number one thing that I delivered people from (rheumatoid arthritis) come upon me' (Sumrall, 1995). It was a lonely death. Many of the leaders he had helped establish congregations and construct church buildings, now turned their backs on him.

His brother George died in 1962, spending his final years in seclusion as he pursued the idea that England was one of the lost tribes of Israel. Both men ended their days amid enduring controversy and rumours, yet their faith and devotion rubbed off onto Edward. His father and uncle taught him to radically pursue the faith, even if it meant swimming against the tide.

The Jefferies brothers were unconventional ministers who bucked the system, disturbing some of the established ways of thinking about mission. Their church planting and healing crusades publicly demonstrated God's power and led to many leaps of faith into the great unknown. Sometimes they fell flat on their faces, but when that happened they just got up and brushed the dust from off their clothes.

They passed these lessons on, as Edward Jeffries so clearly testified. When asked to what he attributed the success of the 1934 Liverpool crusades, in typical Jeffries fashion he responded that it was entirely down to faith and prayer. It was a moment in time when God said, 'Go,' and he simply went.

Thoughts

> We didn't count on suffering, we didn't count on pain, but
> if the blessing's in the valley, then in the river I will wait.
> Find me in the river, find me there. Find me on my knees
> with my soul laid bare ... I've walked against the water,
> now I'm waiting if you please.

(Martin Smith: *Find Me in the River*)

It would take volumes to describe the lives of the Jeffries, men of God whose impact on this nation is still seen today. The congregations they helped establish, the network of relationships that were rooted in their works, and the style of meetings they conducted continue to shape ideas of mission. These servants of the Gospel truly shook this land and beyond.

There are many stories of astounding crusade meetings where bones were heard clicking into place, sickness was boldly ordered to depart, and limbs grew right before the eyes of the watching congregation. There were no tricks or illusions, just an immediate and visible change in the musculoskeletal system that could not be explained other than through God's divine touch.

Over the years the Jeffries brothers would share fellowship with names well known within the chapters of faith: Dr. Martyn Lloyd-Jones, the Welsh evangelical minister at Westminster Chapel, London, and Mrs. Catherine Booth-Clibborn, the eldest daughter of the Salvation Army founders, to name but two. In the brothers' dying days, Dr. Lester Sumrall spent prayerful moments with Stephen, and a young evangelist by the name of Reinhard Bonnke stumbled across George's house on a London visit that ended in a worldwide commission.

The Jeffries were great evangelists in a nation that was beginning to question faith. Their crusades rivalled those of D.L. Moody and Dr. Torrey; their sermons cut through the hardest of hearts. Yet a simple and powerful story dances through each astounding demonstration of faith.

These men paid a personal price: even in the heights of success, behind closed doors they embraced a heart attitude of following the Spirit's prompting. Sometimes the consequence was rejection from others or an internal cost when things just didn't make earthly sense. But their path of submission, demonstrated that trust in God is more than words; it is an expression of obedience that rarely gets public praise.

The black and white image of the first 'Wooden Cathedral' gathering held by Edward depicts a meeting hall, full of expectant faces of all ages. The background story of this snapshot is sacrificial acts, prayerful cries at midnight, obedience guiding the pilgrim on rocky paths.

It is a journey that never cries for attention, yet demands the fullness of a love filled heart. The fruit of each step is ever lasting, providing nourishment and refreshment for every pilgrim of faith. And as only God's creating Hand can do, the passage of time cannot restrict its effect. Because caught within the testimony of my family line, is a loved one who found themselves with bended knees at the front of a Jeffries' crusade meeting.

The righteous rocker

Today, so many people ask me if I can tell them how they can start
or enter into a music ministry . . . My answer to their question is
almost always the same. 'Are you willing to never play music again?
Are you willing to be a nothing? Are you willing to go anywhere and
do anything for Christ? Are you willing to stay right where you are
and let the Lord do great things through you, though no one may
seem to notice at all?' They all seem to answer each of those
questions with a quick 'Yes!' But I really doubt if they
know what their answer entails.

(Keith Green: *So You Wanna Be a Rock Star*)

The writers knew that what they had crafted was something special,
a creative piece of work that the music world had never seen before.
They had planned its release carefully, with previews before the cut-off
date for the Tony awards in 1968. Yet for some reason the award
organisers brought forward the deadline which meant that the show
missed out on any prizes.

This hurdle of opposition wasn't new to the writing team. The
musical was a daring American production, pushing the boundaries
of acceptable theatre topics by introducing controversial news items.
The 'rock musical' reflected youth culture through contemporary songs
and audience participation, and the new genre it created provoked
mixed reactions from the established giants of the scene. *Ziegfeld
Follies* had explored the same line of thought with its creative take on
the infamous Parisian music hall, a decade earlier, but this latest
musical expression took the concept to a whole new level.

What shocked the established ranks more than anything else
was the political commentary on the hippie movement and the
Vietnam War. It told the story of a counter-culture mixed-race group
of youths using the weapons of the sexual revolution to question
sacred national symbols.

The narrative followed the struggles of two young friends, George
Berger and Claude Bukowski, seeking to swim against the tide of society.
Eventually Claude, unable to resist the pressure that his parents and
the world were placing upon him, accepts the draft for Vietnam. In an
emotional final scene, George calls out for his missing friend, failing
to recognise him in army uniform with his hair neatly cut. Claude

marches off to war, and the protest dwindles away. As everyone leaves the stage, the former hippie rebel lies dead, killed in a war he once protested against.

Hair was more than a musical, it was a political statement, and its title drew attention to two opposing ways of living. Its launch in London provoked the same mixed response within the British crowds. The opening of the musical was one day after the abolition of the theatre censorship act, enacted in 1737 to prevent political satire and commentary. Times columnist Irving Wardle noted, 'Nothing else remotely like it has struck the West End. Its honesty and passion give it the quality of a truly theatrical celebration, the joyous sound of a group of people telling the world exactly what they feel.' (Wardle, 1968)

This was the beginning of an interesting theatrical run and a film adaptation of the same name. Each production heralded stars in the making, propelling their names onto a platform of theatrical awards and global recognition. One emerging star auditioned for a role in this controversial musical in 1969.

His name was Larry Norman and he had already enjoyed fame with a hit song in 1968, and opening up concerts for stars such as Van Morrison, The Doors, Jimi Hendrix and The Who. But his experiences with the heroes of this emerging music scene, were of disappointment and confusion. Many times Larry would see the champions of this 'love and rock 'n' roll revolution' as far from their public persona. His recollection of a depressed Janis Joplin sipping whisky from a paper cup exemplified this contradictory world for him, which he framed in his groundbreaking album *Only Visiting this Planet*.

Being raised in a strict Christian family who had encouraged him to shun any form of musical activity outside of the church had left a mark on his life. As a budding songwriter in his early youth, he found an outlet through mission work, encouraged by his father. But like his musical hero Elvis Presley, the musical beat that he was hearing within, struggled to find a voice within traditional Christian America.

After giving up college, Norman threw himself into the music scene, finding the early stages of success that led him to the theatre door of *Hair*. The storyline of characters fighting against the conservative agenda was not lost on this young man, and the producers saw the relevance, offering him one of the lead roles as Berger, the rebel who passionately battled against the system.

It was an amazing offer, especially as his friend was to also be cast as Claude, the other lead. With fame and fortune attached to such a role, it would be hard for any young man to turn their back on it, but Norman did. A year earlier he had a spiritual encounter that had challenged his thoughts about life. Unsure of whether to use his musical talent back within the Christian scene, or continue to venture into 'worldly' realms, he was faced with a real life decision as he stared at the dotted line of a contract that would surely put his name in lights.

Norman knew the message of the musical. He had experienced the tension of swimming against the tide. Yet he also knew from his encounter with the Holy Spirit that the answer to the issues being raised wasn't what was being promoted in its finale. His decision to turn down the role was met with confusion and reproach, particularly from his friend who accepted his own offer and would later win a theatrical award. Norman went back to his apartment in tears, questioning his direction once again. It was to be one of the hardest decisions of his life, and one that remained a painful cross until his death in 2008.

The months that followed led to deep soul-searching, while he expressed his convictions through street and social mission work. Still unable to satisfy his desire for the Christian message to be communicated in music outside of the confines of church programmes, he stumbled into a coffeehouse that dared to host rock bands playing songs that spoke about Jesus. These bands were part of an emerging grassroots movement of faith that was slowly filtering through America, expressed through the counter-cultural hippies.

Motivated by the radical message of devotion to Christ's return, this group of rejects and misfits started to form faith communes for mission and Biblical living. Taking a direct and sometimes blunt approach to Scripture, they tapped into a youth culture looking for answers away from the established structures. With Jesus being presented as the One True Rebel by long-haired disciples, its uncompromising message gathered momentum and soon filtered out from its birthplace on the West Coast.

This was the 'Jesus Movement': a collection of radical 'Jesus Freaks' who shook the foundations of the constructs people had built around the Christian message. Arthur Blessitt chained himself to a twelve-foot cross for twenty-eight days, and walked across America and then the world with the provocative symbol of faith. His determination to obey his Lord and make the Gospel message real and tangible, led him to be arrested, mugged and threatened with death many times. Yet his stark commitment to evangelism led to numerous prayers for salvation, from the street gutter to the wealthiest of palaces.

Then there was the controversial musician Keith Green, whose direct and uncompromising talk was backed up by an intense lifestyle determined to echo that of Christ. His passion to re-image the music industry led him to not charge for his concerts and give away his music for whatever donation people would pay.

Backed by a record company manager who understood what he was trying to achieve, and a database of names and addresses collected wherever he went, his message that 'Jesus commands us to go' encouraged a growth in mission. It also challenged fellow artists to reconsider their own practices, and sometimes view him as the black sheep of the Christian music industry.

Barry McGuire, Phil Keaggy, Second Chapter of Acts, Randy Stonehill, Chuck Smith and the hippie prophet Lonnie Frisbee are just a few names in the long list that these pages cannot fully capture. As with any pioneer movement, daring to go places avoided by established groups, there were casualties, scandals and questionable lifestyle choices. Ironically, the practices of some of these groups eventually provoked the emergence of the shepherding ideology, a form of control with Scriptural language attached to it.

But we must not underestimate the effects of a small group of misfit hippies who met in coffeehouses and wouldn't keep silent about the issues of their day. Their approach to life and outworking of faith was slowly but surely changing the footprint of the church. Larry Norman stood in one of these Christian coffeehouses, listening to a band mix rock tunes and the Gospel message. He later created his first album Upon this Rock, which was branded a new form of pornography by some ministers who thought it blasphemous to combine Jesus with the music of the world.

Whatever upset he caused from his first recording was nothing compared to his next production. His 1972 album *Only Visiting This Planet* carried tracks like *Why Should the Devil Have All the Good Music?*, *Righteous Rocker* and *I Wish We'd All Been Ready*. He challenged Christians to re-imagine the mission field in a unified music scene, bringing the raw reality of life directly to the feet of anyone who would listen.

He was a man who wouldn't let anyone off the hook. A rocker on the outside but a broken pilgrim within, he heard his Lover's call and counted its precious cost.

Thoughts

Sipping whiskey from a paper cup, you drown your sorrows
till you can't stand up. Take a look at what you've done to yourself;
you put the bottle back on the shelf. Yellow finger from your
cigarettes, your hands are shaking while your body sweats.
Why don't you look into Jesus, he's got the answer.

Gonorrhoea on Valentine's Day, and you're still looking for the
perfect lay. You think rock and roll will set you free, honey;
you'll be dead before you're thirty-three. Shooting junk till
you're half insane, broken needle in your purple vein.

Why don't you look into Jesus, he's got the answer.

(Larry Norman: *Why Don't You Look into Jesus*)

Larry Norman watched the legendary singer Janis Joplin back stage and saw a broken and bitter hidden life that countered the image she was about to present. He later witnessed famous and adored bands speaking of love and peace to their worshipping audience, and then abusing and fighting each other behind closed doors. The idols of a music revolution declared a radical message of unity and acceptance, but lived like chameleons in a world that rarely declared its true colours.

It's not unusual for the public persona to differ with the hidden reality. The world pressures us to wear varied masks, all amplifying image through what we buy and the stories we tell.

The path of obedience confronts contradictions in pilgrims of faith who are also frail creatures with feet of clay. Honesty exposes the truth and cuts through illusion like a two-edged sword. It begins in the heart, a broken ground of devotion that nourishes fragile roots. Beyond the hidden life of the prayer closet, we must open our lives in vulnerability, yet not shy away from speaking out the reality of what we see.

The cries of justice from a broken heart sound different to opinionated and arrogant howls. The frailty of Larry's own life was plain for him and his fellow travellers to see, yet his devotion to God continually addressed the personal contradictions. His boldness to declare the truth to a world that preferred a lie, meant that some shunned or rejected his message.

Yet he continued to press forward, leaving precious footprints on the pilgrim path we now tread. Through his lyrics on his *Only Visiting*

This Planet album he dared to speak out against the mask of illusion many happily wore:

> Rolling Stones are millionaires, flower children pallbearers, Beatles said 'All you need is love', and then they broke up. Jimi took an overdose, Janis followed so close, the whole music scene and all the bands are pretty comatose. This time last year, people didn't wanna hear. They looked at Jesus from afar, this year he's a 'superstar.'

> . . . your money says in God we trust, but it's against the law to pray in school. You say we beat the Russians to the moon and I say you starved your children to do it. You say all men are equal, all men are brothers, then why are the rich more equal than others. Don't ask me for the answer, I've only got one. That a man leaves his darkness when he follows the Son.

Note 'F'
The marvel of daily life

Introduction: Every little thing we do

You're picking up toys on the living room floor for the 15th
time today. Match up socks and sweeping up lost Cheerios
that got away. You put a baby on your hip and colour on
your lips, and head out the door.

Maybe you're that guy with the suit and tie, maybe your
shirt says your name. You may be hooking up mergers,
cooking up burgers. But at the end of the day, little stuff,
in between stuff. God sees it all the same.

Do everything you do to the glory of the One who made you,
every little thing that you do to bring a smile to His face.
And tell the story of grace with every move that you make.

(Steven Curtis Chapman: *Do Everything*)

It started off as a normal morning as a couple rose and got ready
for the day ahead. The sporadic chat as the checklist of 'things to
remember' was mentally ticked off revealed a deep love for each
other. As husband and wife they had seen many highs and lows. The
joy of finding each other, creating a home and pursuing their dreams
together, had brought them many precious experiences. Yet one
dream remained unfilled, continually leading them to the valley of
tears and questions.

A cloud of disappointment surrounded aspirations for a child of their own. Over a timeline of weeks, months and years, prayers of hope echoed in the silence of unanswered replies. As old age finally caught up with them, it hammered the final nail on the coffin of a fragile dream. What at first seemed too heavy to bear had now become normal, entwined in peaceful acceptance that it was simply not meant to be. They filled in the space of what was missing by serving the community, and their standing grew as the husband took the role of a priestly mediator between the God of the universe and his creation.

Without fanfare, they said goodbye as the man set off for the temple. Routine conversation gave way to a general hush as it was time to draw lots to see who would represent the people through the act of devotion in the temple. Though familiar in their daily routine, it was an awesome moment. The series of words was engrained in their memories, but this moment of seeking God's guidance was always held in high regard. And this time the lot was cast on the childless husband.

He went about his priestly duty, every step performing a habit embedded in his mind, when without warning he was confronted with an angel telling him, 'Do not be afraid'. What was then spoken changed his life forever. A long-term prayer for fatherhood had now been miraculously answered.

The angel spoke of a boy who would be called John, and would live a particular lifestyle from childhood. This heavenly declaration hinted at the unique path that this child would eventually travel. What had begun as an ordinary day revealed the answer to a couple's prayer and a nation's hope.

The life of Zechariah and Elizabeth reminds me of an interview I did some years ago. Sitting on an uncomfortable wooden pew in a Scottish church building, I listened to a handful of people tell me their experiences of living through revival. Despite the diversity of their personal journeys, the common factor was how the mundane routine of life became entwined with the suddenness of the divine. The sacred and secular merged in the blurred edges of time.

At first I found the conversations frustrating, as I wanted to focus on dramatic scenes of miraculous power, not on tales about the price of milk or school meetings. Yet as the hours moved on, I began to see their narratives in a different light. Each of these pilgrims expressed how heavenly signs were mingled with everyday living. Their commitment to family and community service was as much of a demonstration of devotion as when they knelt in adoration at a revival meeting.

Their stories never diminished the preciousness of Christ's touch. Their tales described a divine embrace between humanity and the celestial realm, with God's kingdom very much at hand. Two parallel journeys, merged into a path of glory where the present dances with the future, and prayerful hopes become reality.

Revival history eloquently testifies to this beautiful intimacy of worship and devotion expressed in ordinary life. The 18th-century Church of England minister Griffith Jones observed how illiteracy affected his Welsh town as he chatted to his parishioners. Unable to ignore this, he prayerfully considered a project that would go on to radically change the approach to education. Aware that the Welsh language was neglected in literature, he embarked on a journey to address this imbalance.

Building on the early ideas of the Society for Promoting Christian Knowledge (SPCK), which was exploring ways of providing education through Christian material, Jones developed the work of 'Circulating Schools'. This radical approach provided free education to the poor through the publication of Welsh Bibles. In homes, church buildings and business premises, an unconventional new school system affected whole families as they began to enjoy the precious gift of learning.

It is estimated that by the time of Jones' death, nearly a quarter of a million people in Wales had learned to read and write. His primary concern was not the preservation of the Welsh language but the most helpful tongue that would promote the Gospel message. But his investment into the native dialect amplified the Welsh vernacular at a time when the English tongue was being heavily promoted by the church and educated fellows. It would be too simplistic to say that this work safeguarded a language from a possible extinction, but what it did help to achieve was a new movement of literature and spoken word that praised the voice of the people. Something that helped support writers, poets and folk singers to take the stories of faith and praise them within their treasured culture. It was a movement that captured local expression and rising wisdom within a land that was seeing the early rays of revival. Jones was a *"man who broke forth a little before the break of dawn (revival) . . . A bright, glorious star, shining amid the night's threatening clouds, a man whose clear trumpet call was heard by many . . . In time, (his) home at Llanddowror became a virtual school of the prophets."* (Jones, 1902).

One of those affected was a young man by the name of Daniel Rowland, who became a prominent preacher in the 18th-century Welsh Revival. A passionate and energetic evangelist, he travelled over 150,000 miles on foot or horseback in his lifetime, proclaiming the message in every valley of his treasured land.

A 15-year old girl called Mary Jones was schooled through this unconventional movement. By the late 18th century, non-conformist minister Thomas Charles had developed the work further with help of philanthropists like Charles Grant, who was chairman of the British East India Company, and the politician William Wilberforce. Building local networks and encouraging funding from congregations and business groups, their efforts spurred a sense of responsibility for the education and wellbeing of the whole community.

Mary Jones started to learn to read through the Welsh Bible, and because of her desire to learn more of God's Word, she saved money for nearly six years to buy her own copy. At that time it was still rare to have the Holy Scriptures on a living room bookshelf, and in many areas the only copy to be found was the Circulating School's own prized edition. Mary' 26-mile walk to obtain her Bible, which affected Charles so profoundly that he went back to the Council of the Religious Tract Society to share the challenge of finding more effective means of distributing Bibles. The story of Mary's pilgrimage contributed into a wider dialogue already taking place, eventually giving rise to the creation of the Bible Society.

The power of the divine within the mundane is no better noted than the story of Granville Sharp in 1765. An ordinary visit to his brother's medical practice in London led him to a doorstep encounter with a black slave called Jonathan Strong. This slave had been severely beaten and flogged by his master, and then abandoned on the streets and left to die. Covering the bills for his medical care, Granville and his brother oversaw his treatment and eventually helped him find employment in the city.

Two years later Jonathan's old master tracked him down and attempted to kidnap him with the aim of selling him on. Realising that the law favoured the rights of the master, Granville committed himself to pursuing reform. This was not an easy task, as he had no background in the legal profession. His commitment to the cause eventually led to the case being won, and Jonathan lived as a free man for another five years before his death from past injuries.

From that point on, Granville determined to confront the issue of slavery, networking with the call for social justice emerging from some of the revival preachers of the day. His concerted efforts led to him becoming known as the 'Grand Old Man' of the abolition cause that would eventually have its day in the Houses of Parliament.

This movement also challenged Charles Finney to include its message of human freedom into his sermons, tying the message of salvation with people's responsibility not to enslave others. He developed the 'altar call', still practiced in churches today, but with a twist involving a practical demonstration of compassion, so that those 'saved' would also become signed-up members of the abolition movement.

These revival narratives are full of staggering figures and marvellous anecdotes: an education movement impacting on a vast number of Welsh citizens; preaching that spurred a young man to grow into one of the most famous Welsh revivalists of the 18th century; commitment to share the Scriptures through the world, provoked by young girl's action; and an abolition network connecting faith with social responsibility.

It is amazing to see the context of these dramatic scenes of God's work: a minister's walk through town changing the course of his life forever; an education system that challenged a young man to shake Wales; a non-conformist minister opening up his home to teach others to read and write.

A fifteen-year-old girl who so treasured the Scriptures that she travelled a great distance to find a copy of her own, unaware that her actions would create a ripple effect still seen today. Nor did a man think that a routine visit to his brother would change his life's focus and that of the statute books.

We simply don't know the wonders being declared in the throne room of God. Zechariah and Elizabeth were unaware of being seen from heaven as being *'righteous in the sight of God'*, as they observed all of *'the Lord's commands and decrees blamelessly'*. The same could be said of Griffith Jones, Thomas Charles, Mary Jones, Granville Sharpe and many others in the annals of revival history.

Our stories usually focus on one special day, for example, the dramatic moments when an angel appears or a project finds success. But let us not forget devotion in the routines of life which is never out of God's sight.

This is the story within revival, a narrative of daily living that carries a worth beyond words. Where pilgrims of faith walk a path that is both mundane and miraculous, challenging our preference of just the mountain-top experiences. What marvels and astounds also finds home within the cherished gem we call life. Where every breath that we take contributes to a work that one day may just leave us speechless.

Not the plan

Life is what happens to you while you're busy making other plans.

(John Lennon: *Beautiful Boy*)

A well thought-out plan can make perfect sense to its architect, hopefully with perfect continuity between the original dream and its realisation. For Dwight Moody, his careful deliberation and intricate design seemed to offer an ideal solution to a problem at hand. For a couple of years since 1861 he had worked in Chicago with the Young Men's Christian Association (YMCA), and had seen it develop in both stature and recognition. Yet its growth had also challenged the very heart of its constitution, with its ethos needing to be balanced with the demands of differing agendas.

Moody was fully aware of the history of this movement, how it had responded to a need in society with genuine acts of compassion. But since its humble inception the world had changed, and Moody believed the moment was ripe to once more venture into the unknown, to remould this beloved work in response to the challenges provoked by these new times.

The YMCA was founded in Victorian England in 1844 by a twenty-two-year-old draper called George Williams and eleven friends, who wanted to encourage young men in the ways of healthy citizenship. For some time they had seen the temptations of a bustling industrial city, and realised that for young Christians like themselves to grow in their faith, they needed to encourage one another in practical living.

What emerged was a fellowship group, a space that welcomed all by subverting some of the social barriers of a strict English class system. In 1851, a marine missionary called Thomas Sullivan took the YMCA to America, and over the following years this growing international work developed into affordable lodging, language programmes, skills development, leadership courses and health education.

As Moody travelled to the YMCA International Convention in 1870 this was not just head knowledge, but an active awareness deep in his heart. Three years earlier, he had sought out George Williams during his first UK trip and had enjoyed the privilege of sharing stories, prayers and fellowship with the founder of the work he so deeply respected. First-hand he caught the spirit of the original aims, saw the fire in William's eyes and heard the passion in his voice. Laid out on a verbal canvas was the timeline of its early history, painted with the colours from the founder's brush.

By the end of their conversation, this living painting had embedded itself in the heart of the young Moody. He understood the daring dream and the uncompromising journey. Now, three years later, he was to deliver a plan to the convention that would once again highlight the spirit of that radical approach.

Over time he had observed that some of the Victorian principles that had once served them so well, had become outdated. Its strict disciplinary code and separation of the sexes made sense in the early context, but its current enforcement had become a hindrance instead of the means of achieving an ultimate goal. The rules that governed the work were no longer empowering its young people to swim against the tide of spiritual compromise.

It was now time for the mission to once again pioneer new ways of living out faith. Moody felt that the radical message he was to bring honoured the YMCA's history but the carefully laid out plan he presented was soon dismantled, as the International chairman quickly dismissed any changes and moved onto the next point.

This was a major blow for Moody, as the central purpose for him coming to the convention was to pioneer a new dream. Yet with a swift change of agenda, he now saw his objective in ruins. It's hard to drag oneself up from the ground after such a quick and decisive knock down, and the dismissal of such a cherished plan led Moody to re-examine the burning passion he had within his heart. Had he read the signs wrong? Were his thoughts misdirected?

He pondered these questions like a sombre traveller who had lost his way and his excitement for the rest of the convention was dulled. Yet sometimes the most simple and inconspicuous of actions lead to a heavenly crescendo that requires a different type of listening, and during a morning-prayer meeting at the 1870 Convention one such moment happened for Moody.

It was a strange prayer meeting, with long, drawn-out prayers and truly awful singing. Those who yearned to worship were aware that time was passing. One attendee saw a glimmer of hope as a meticulously attired gentleman turned up late. As he sat down amid a prayer that had been in full flow for what seemed like an eternity, his neighbour whispered, 'The singing here has been abominable. I wish you would start up something when that man stops praying, if he ever does' (Pollock, 1963). The plea was answered as the well-groomed gentleman stood up and led the entire group in song.

As the meeting drew to a close, the singer was introduced to Moody. With minimal words, Moody asked this man three questions: 'Where are you from? Are you married? What is your business?' The response was as swift as the questions themselves. 'New Castle, Pennsylvania. I am married, two children. In government service, the Revenue'. It was a response that brought a gleeful reply from Moody. 'You will have to give that up . . . come to Chicago and help me in my work' (ibid, 1963).

Both the conversation and its conclusion was not what the singer expected, and the prospect of giving up a highly respected job along with its steady income was not the easiest of decisions. He agreed in prayer to consider the offer, then each departed for the rest of the day.

The following afternoon the singer received a note from Moody, asking him to join him on a street corner, and though an unusual request, he couldn't resist responding to the mysterious invitation. On arrival, Moody greeted him with heartfelt enthusiasm, and proudly displayed a scruffy soapbox. As the workers from a nearby factory left their shifts to return home, this sophisticated man was directed to stand on the box and start singing to those who passed by.

The singer's name was Ira David Sankey, and in years to come he would be called the 'Sweet Singer of Methodism'. He touched the hardest of hearts by composing lyrics and tunes that captured the beauty of sacrificial service and prayer. His later writing partnership with the blind composer of *Blessed Assurance*, Fanny Crosby, painted landscapes of Christ's love beyond earthly sight. And by the time he was called to his heavenly home in 1908, Sankey left a heavenly fragrance for all to breathe, captured in exquisite poetry.

Moody and Sankey formed a partnership that travelled an estimated million miles, preaching the gospel of love to over one hundred million people. It would go down in history as one of the most successful evangelistic collaborations ever recorded. Their pioneering approach to mission work echoed some of the earlier values of George Williams and the YMCA in challenging social barriers, exploring ways of Bible distribution, developing networks of relational groups, and encouraging people to swim against the tide of conformity.

From an unpromising meeting, a lifelong friendship resulted and the gospel was brought to a new generation.

Thoughts

> Blessed assurance, Jesus is mine. Oh what a foretaste
> of glory divine. Heir of salvation, purchase of God,
> born of His Spirit, washed in His blood.

This is my story this is my song, praising my Saviour all the day long.

(Francis J. Crosby: *Blessed Assurance*)

I have lost count of the times when my carefully laid plans have finished up broken on the floor of unpredicted outcomes. All kinds of unexpected changes have disrupted what I assumed was an airtight proposition that covered each developing stage of a project. So I feel sympathy for Moody in his failed plan with the YMCA.

He had a logical proposal to adapt the mission to reflect changing times in society. So often our plans make sense, and naturally we believe that the architect is always right. In our mind there are signposts to important things that need to be achieved. For Moody, one such marker was the convention of 1870.

This was the moment when his passion for the work and detailed agenda would be presented to its worldwide committee. He proposed to map out the future steps of the YMCA, exciting the hearts of leaders and workers alike with new forms of evangelism that would take the world by storm. Yet Moody soon discovered that the divine signposts that God places along our pilgrimage can be different to the ones we choose.

His connection with the song-smith called Sankey opened up a whole new landscape of missionary work. This development was completely off his road map, yet God connected them as a beautifully crafted signpost pointing towards a future of creative freedom. This was not about a restructure of the YMCA or any programme initiative, but the remodelling of Moody's own life. The steps he was about to take could not be seen through the eyes of man, but only grasped through the beating of a worshiping heart.

Our Creator carefully crafts his divine plans in the hearts and minds of his loved ones. He doesn't expect us to know every detail of the route but to lean on a beautiful truth – the 'blessed assurance' that he is in control.

His hints are not always easy to follow. Sometimes we get it right; sometimes we misinterpret them. But oh, what an exciting prospect it is, that even when our plans are torn to pieces we may be led to our own frustrating prayer meeting.

To live the life

Many are the words we speak, many are the songs we sing. Many kinds of offerings, but now to live the life. All we want to do is bring you something real, bring you something true.

Now to go the extra mile, now to turn the other cheek, and to serve you with a life. Let us share your fellowship, even of your suffering. Never let the passion die, now to live the life.

(Matt Redman: *Now to Live the Life*)

During the 19th century, both the population and industry of London were growing dramatically, yet were not in harmonious balance. Over the space of sixty years, the city's population had grown by nearly four million, reaching the staggering figure of five and a half million. Nearly three million were unemployed, with roughly half of those living in abject poverty. Those on the lower rungs of the employment ladder had a dire existence of long working hours in harsh sweatshops, even if more privileged workers enjoyed education and healthcare. There was a vast discrepancy of experience in the so-called glorious industrial age.

A growing moral unease arose in Victorian England about this prejudicial employment ladder. The pioneering sermons of the previous century's Methodist and Quaker preachers had left the nation's conscience with a message of ethics and justice, and increasing numbers of people could not escape that personal challenge. This was now bearing fruit in proactive stances of compassion and faith.

An Anglican clergyman by the name of Samuel Barnett and his wife, Henrietta were sacrificially addressing the poor conditions around them by providing evening education. At this time, the controversial Poor Law sought to provide jobs for those in needs by moving them from rural to urban areas. Although poverty was eased through the re-distribution of wealth and self-empowerment, as we have already seen in the story of Dickens, the increased demand for workhouses had horrendous consequences.

This compassionate couple's demand for solutions inspired a dream that some thought impossible to achieve in the poverty-stricken slums of England. Their beautiful hope was that both rich and poor could live harmoniously together, interdependent and with a value for every life. They believed that by creating a space where all could share their experiences and talents, everyone regardless of status or gender could work collectively for the betterment of the whole.

This dream had a name, the 'Settlement Movement', and very quickly divided opinion. It encouraged the better-off to move into the inner-cities, to live, work, share and co-partner initiatives. Some saw a wonderful opportunity to stimulate learning, art, sports and craftsmanship in the slums, but critics called it cultural imperialism, the rich and educated dominating the poor by coming in as experts and keepers of creative abilities.

The debate gathered intensity as the months moved into years, but it never stopped the work on the ground. A group of people were trying desperately hard to develop a new space where gaps were bridged by mutual respect as the disadvantaged were linked with future leaders and shapers of industry. This daring idea could pave a way for those on the path to government and commerce to bring the needs of the forgotten to the forefront of politics and society. It was an idea which truly did succeed.

During those early years, a young middle-class couple along with their baby daughter felt compelled to support the Settlement goals with an active hope of seeing change in society. Henry and Margaret Nevinson chose to share their family life with the poor, and their path was shaped by the rawness of what they saw and experienced first hand. They were authors, suffragette campaigners and co-founders of the 'Men's League for Women's Suffrage'.

Henry was a noted war correspondent, particularly for his reporting of the Second Boer War and its concentration camps. He would also write *Thames Stories*, later titled *Neighbours of Ours*: a collection of tales about London's poor that attempted, like Dickens, to expose the rich and comfortable to the reality of the alleyways.

Over time they lived in different locations, but their heart for justice never altered. *Harpers* Monthly Magazine hired Henry to investigate rumours of slavery in the cocoa bean industry of Angola. The Cadbury's family were shocked to hear that a core value of their Quaker faith of the sanctity of human life was being abused in the chocolate business they had created.

Henry went to Luanda, Angola to independently examine the stories that were emerging from the villages, specifically about the cover-up by authorities and business groups who were safeguarding their profits. He met an impasse, with many people refusing to help him or answer any of his questions, and soon realised that many lived in fear for their own lives if they entertained the visiting journalist.

Undeterred, he ventured inland, on a treacherous journey like a 'goat-path in the Alps in a land of bare and rugged hills, deeply scarred by weather and full of wild and brilliant colours' (Nevinson, 1906). This 450-mile trek eventually started to uncover the hidden story. Henry came across discarded shackles:

> I saw several hundreds of them ... scattered up and down the path ... strewn with dead men's bones ... the skeletons of slaves who were unable to keep up with the march and so were murdered or left to die (ibid, 1906).

This began a flood of information as Henry pieced together the complex picture of people being sold into slavery due to debt, family issues, accusations of witchcraft and internal power struggles. Despite the Slavery Abolition Act of 1833, he witnessed how authorities, corporations and government were finding loopholes to continue the trade in human beings. He noted that someone's status could be officially changed from 'slave' to 'volunteer worker', yet their daily existence would still be that of a slave. It was an insight he refused to keep quiet about.

Nevinson's six-month investigation appeared in the August 1905 edition of *Harpers* Monthly magazine; concluding that 'the whole question of African slavery is still before us' (idid, 1906). The discovery of legalised slavery shocked readers and the chocolate firms of Cadbury, Rowntree and Fry. What followed was a prolonged and painful journey for those company directors, as they tackled how best to eradicate such injustice. Their goal was not fully realised, but their business practices modelled new ways of operating now embodied in some of the latest initiatives in fair trade and anti-slavery campaigns.

Other individuals who engaged with the Settlement Movement were William Beveridge and Clement Attlee. Their exposure and investment in this work before their famous days in politics, contributed to their passion for social reform against the evils of 'want, disease, ignorance, squalor and idleness'. Beveridge's report, *Social Insurance and Allied Services*, became a strong foundation of Attlee's Labour Party policy when they entered government in 1945.

The famous 'cradle to the grave' Welfare State was formed, based upon three pillars of hope. A 'free at the point of use' National Health Service, full employment, and family support, regardless of status. Although not perfect, and perhaps somewhat paternalistic, the impact on the nation's health and social care has been great and lasting.

There were many diverse expressions of the ideas behind the Settlement Movement, but all encompass the hope that small human actions can bring about big change. This movement was a bridge from grassroots activism to shifts in governmental policy and economic practice. Its greatest legacy is the notion that a humble idea worked and is still being lived out to this very day – now to live the life.

Thoughts

He leadeath me, He leadeth me. By His own hand, He leadeth me.
His faithful follower, I would be. For by His hand He leadeth me.

(Words by Joseph Gilmore,
Music by William Bradbury: He Leadeth Me)

The comforting hymn *He Leadeth Me* was written during the height of the American Civil War by a young man inspired by the words of the 23rd Psalm. Amid fear and uncertainty, blood and loss, Joseph Gilmore lent upon the surety of God's leading Hand. He described as best as he could the beauty found in trust, a profound dimension of our spiritual relationship that goes beyond that of just obedience.

Matthew's gospel has the powerful account of a disciple's faithful obedience. In response to Jesus' invitation to *'Come'*, Simon Peter stepped out of a boat and attempted to walk on water. Christ's followers today still step into the unknown with acts of committed faith that encourage us to grow stronger every day. Yet it's often hard for us to step out in trust when we see the rolling waves around us, when our senses and inner logic say that there must be another way.

The words of Jesus must have reminded Peter of that moment when a stranger asked him to lay down his nets and become a fisher of men. This call infiltrated every aspect of his life: his profession, his income, his friends and his purpose. His acts of obedience culminated in the big challenge of walking on water.

Trust in God affects each deed and decision of life. Whether defying the law of gravity or speaking words that expose the sin of slavery, it is expressed in the dramatic and the mundane, both publicly and in our inner attitude. The significant issue is whether we are being guided through our journey by God's leading hand.

A mother's story

When I lose my way and I forget my name, remind me who
I am. In the mirror all I see is who I don't wanna be, remind
me who I am. When my heart is like a stone and I'm
running far from home, remind me who I am.

In the loneliest places, when I can't remember what grace is.
Tell me once again who I am to you, that I belong to you.

(Jason Gray: *Remind Me Who I Am*)

The year was 1851 and Victorian Britain was displaying exhibits of majestic grandeur before an expectant crowd. Housed in a temporary crystal structure, this glistening palace of light stood proudly on the fields of Hyde Park, London. It shone the beacon of human creativity to over six million people who would pass through its welcoming doors.

The 'World's Greatest Fair' had created an excited buzz on the streets of London during its opening month in May. Although all the tickets had been pre-sold, a flood of extra visitors made their way to the elaborate city gardens, to gaze on a construction that was a visual marvel. Yet among the crowds that were drawn like moths to a flame, walked a solitary figure in the opposite direction. This man's mind was firmly fixed on something other than human constructions.

This 30-year-old lone gentleman, John Hambleton, had lived a hectic existence. Running away from his Liverpool home at the age of fourteen, he emigrated to Australia to seek the acclaim of stage lights and performance. But having faced the harsh reality of the theatrical life, he glimpsed a ray of hope when he heard news of the Californian gold rush. Travelling over to America, he became a gold digger by day and an actor by night.

This adjustment wasn't easy as he juggled his fragile career. A one-man tour across the States led him many times to run for his life from town to town, hunted by bandits and hit men that he had upset with questionable business deals or tempted due to a recent successful find. He attempted suicide several times to end his painful journey.

Desperate, angry and shamed, he returned to his home country, and his wandering feet took him past the Crystal Palace, through London's back lanes, finally to stop outside an old bookshop. Taking a long deep breath, he opened the door and ventured inside. There he bought a Bible and began to search through its pages as though he was that gold digger once again.

Nearly four years on, Hambleton stood on a street corner in Liverpool, singing hymns and praying for God's intervention in the city of his childhood. His sister had shared a dream of revival waters running through the streets and soaking into the land he now stood on. Right before his eyes on an early April morning, he saw that dream become a reality.

Rich and poor were praying together, the crescendo of voices almost deafening. This sea of response to a salvation call was a sight to behold: generations together crying out and falling headlong into the Saviour's embrace.

Hambleton truly believed that this was the water of revival running through the streets of Liverpool to a depth never seen before. His desire to preach outdoors had led him to pray for a fellow worker who could complement the Gospel message with song. The answer came in the form of a dockworker called Edward Usher.

Together they favoured a certain lamppost known as the 'Lime Street Lamp' for their prayer meetings, sermons and worship times. They also toured the streets, hunting out drunkards, pointing them towards sobriety, and visiting the sick at home. They had seen some truly marvellous things, but this sight before them on an April morn, was something new and breathtaking.

The flow of revival waters was not a one-time event. Testimonies of salvation became commonplace as Hambleton and Usher toured the country without any itinerary and with little money between them. They simply trusted in the direction of the Holy Spirit, willing to venture into places where few Christians dared to tread. The experiences they faced harked back to Hambleton's gold digging days of old: threats on their lives and fights were commonplace.

As the years went on, they finally parted but were still unified in pursuing the gospel. Usher continued to travel the country in harmony with the wind of the Spirit. Hambleton preached Christ's love wherever possible, with both amazing and terrifying results. As the crowds grew, so did opposition and threats on his life. Because of his determination to challenge the drink houses and gambling dens, he soon found himself facing thugs hired to disrupt his meetings.

As persecution grew, paid informants were tasked with following his movements and spreading false rumours wherever he went. Many expected him to stop preaching or tone down his sermons to appease his accusers. Yet he consistently faced up to the powers that reigned over the dark alleyways, never veering from his quest to see sinners honour the living God.

The famed accounts of the 1859 outpouring in Wales are entwined with the stories of Hambleton and Usher. Despite different denominational expressions, the footprints of these willing servants crossed the borders of the United Kingdom. Yet these moments in time that are treasured within the chronicles of faith, carry a melodic tone that leads us back to a London bookshop in 1851

Hambleton's journey that brought him face to face with a copy of a Bible, finds clarity when placed within his younger years and the continued prayers of a caring mother. His accounts of his mother are bathed with great affection, of how she taught him Scriptures at an early age by interweaving Bible stories with games and imaginary lands.

Hambleton described how her heart was broken as he ran away from home and embraced a life far from the righteous one she had hoped for. Yet it never stopped her belief that one day he would return like the prodigal son. Even though oceans separated them, he could not forget the stories that she had told him as a child, whether in a barren desert or propped up in front of a public bar. The gradual drip feed of love-filled memories eventually led to his decision to come home and visit his family once again.

On returning to Liverpool, Hambleton found that his mother had died some years previously, but before her death had asked one of her daughters to write out a declaration that her son would be saved and come home to serve his Lord. Overwhelmed by that message, he fled again, but in London found himself in a bookshop buying a Bible one day in May 1851.

That purchase was followed by a trail of service to the Gospel that touched countless lives. This wandering preacher never stopped declaring Christ's love in the places that Christendom had forgotten. By the time he died at the age of 69, he had challenged mainstream society with sacrificial love and the richness of grace.

In the last ten years of his life he was blown by the Spirit's wind to the land of his first journey abroad - Australia. Here his path was now shaped by the service of Love and not a rebellious pursuit of selfish gain, as he saw his Lord redeeming every part of his shameful history.

Hambleton's story is a priceless one, but the background of a mother's bedtime story and constant prayer has a humble beauty. Although she never saw the final results of her petitions, the wealth of that investment would reach many lives, such as the philanthropist Thomas Barnardo, who created homes for children in great need, and the 'English Evangelist' Henry Moorhouse, who toured the country distributing Bibles and preaching the Gospel in creative ways. All became converts to Hambleton's belief that the Gospel message carries implications for social responsibility and home life.

It is also worth noting that Moorhouse influenced a young preacher by the name of Dwight Moody. This servant of the gospel message was in years later to be regarded by many as one of the most pioneering evangelists of the 20th century.

Thoughts

When I was a little boy, mama rocked me in her arms.
She protected me from danger, and she kept me safe and warm.

(Kirk Franklin: Mama's Song)

The work of a master craftsman is one of patience and commitment. There are no shortcuts, if the final product is to stand the test of time. To the craftsman, each piece of work has significance beyond public acclaim, but praise is nevertheless welcomed. This desire was obvious with the lavish display of the future, a signal to the watching world that Great Britain was leading the way to a new Utopia. The 'Great Exhibition' of 1851 laid out a vista of technology and challenging ideas, shaking the status quo and praising the bold, inspiring inventors of the day.

The thirteen thousand exhibits on show spoke of hope, ingenuity, beauty and strength, and were viewed by more than six million visitors from across the globe. With tickets in high demand and interest at fever pitch, this amazing money-making exercise helped fund the building of the Victoria and Albert Museum, and the Science Museum, as well as the refurbishment of the Natural History building.

Even the exhibition's housing was a daring work of technology: a beautiful synergy of glass, wood and iron. This wonderful palace of crystal, which claimed its nickname from *Punch Magazine*, shone a light to every guest who graced its doors. This was the future. This was hope, the marvel of humanity's creativity in all its splendour and glory.

In the natural surroundings of Hyde Park, visitors would stare for the first time at a fascinating array in a crystal structure. Birdsong mingled with the collective sound of hushed voices and excited laughter, as visitors walked together towards the light of innovation and imagination. Yet that sparkling entrance leading to a whole new world of creative inspiration reminds me of a display of beauty that overshadowed the most grandiose of palaces.

This was an exhibit of craftsmanship that no draftsman could ever put on paper. The artist was not found in the crystal halls, nor did crowds gather around to stare, but in a nearby bookshop there was a work of breathtaking magnificence. It was a simple act of buying a Bible, enhanced by the craftsmanship of a mother's love.

Note 'G'
The architecture of connections

Introduction: Joining the dots

Again, you can't connect the dots looking forward. You can only connect them looking backwards. So you have to trust that the dots will connect in the future... Because believing that the dots will connect down the road will give you the confidence to follow your heart even when it leads you off the well-worn path.

(Steve Jobs: *Stanford Commencement Speech 2005*)

At the turn of the twentieth century, a travelling evangelist called Reuben Torrey reviewed a manuscript of his collected sermons and lessons. Nuggets of wisdom from his prayer closet and mission work were now collected for others. For years he had faithfully edited the sermons of a well-known preacher for publication, transforming the rough and limited lexicon of the speaker into a river of captivating phrases. He took this discipline seriously, knowing how an error in his editing could alter the essence of what was being said. So he prayerfully crafted each paragraph, after soaking in the preacher's words.

Prayer was a close friend to him. In his early twenties he had devoured the books of two of his favourite authors, Charles Finney and George

Muller. Their attitude of faith had affected him, particularly Muller's testimony of pastoring a church in 1888:

> It seemed my duty to give up my salary and work for God among the poor. So from that day on, every mouthful came directly from my Heavenly Father. There was not a meal on our tables, not a coat on my back, not a dress on my wife's back, not the clothing on the backs of our four children that did not come in answer to prayer. We got everything from God. I was never more serene in my life (Torrey, 1955).

Muller's devotion was echoed by Torrey's passion for evangelism. Spurred by a conversation he had with DL Moody in 1878, he committed that day to always be active in reaching the lost. The preacher encouraged him to learn how to witness by going out and doing it, so he embraced that spirit. From planning to put a Bible in the hands of all he met, to arranging prayer meetings that ended in a commission for mission, he never stopped adjusting, altering and experimenting with varied methods of Gospel witness.

Then a call in 1889 took things to a new level. Moody was now asking him to help spearhead a new venture in mission. Torrey became superintendent of the Chicago Evangelisation Society (to become the Moody Bible Institute), framing its curriculum and selection of staff.

His hands-on approach to the development of its mission programme, alongside his role as editor for Moody's literature, positioned him as the natural successor to the famed evangelist. Some even titled him as the 'Elisha' to the 'Elijah' role of this great preacher: a man who would carry the mantle and receive a double portion of what had gone before. Torrey respected the sincerity of the compliment but continually downplayed his own special role.

Moody's work had set the world alight. He partnered with others to discover new ways of living the gospel message, whether through shared learning from cross-cultural work, or promoting the *Wordless Book* that enabled travelling missionaries to preach the Gospel through visual aids and symbols.

Both Moody and Torrey knew that whatever height they reached, it was only due to previous foundations that had been built. The missionary Hudson Taylor had developed an approach that respected embedded culture and traditions. Charles Spurgeon had used visual aids, later adapted into cards, bracelets and varied wordless books in working with orphans. And these works in turn had been built on the sacrificial service of others.

The early Christian fathers respected the culture of the day, and pious monks mixed art with Scripture. In a collective effort, one pilgrim built upon the devoted service of another. This unity of diverse expression furthered the Gospel message beyond any one person's line of sight.

Torrey had always valued unity and taught his students of evangelism that their work was never made up of just one person's effort. Yet he reached new stature when his friend and fellow worker Moody collapsed during a Kansas City campaign in November 1899. The famed evangelist was taken home, while the assumed successor continued holding successful meetings. A month later Moody died at the age of 62, and the mantle of leadership was passed to the 42-year-old 'Elisha'.

In years to come, Torrey would visit nearly all the corners of the globe, from the dangerous mission fields of China and Japan, to overflowing crowds in Australia and India. By the time of his death in October 1928, he had indeed experienced the double portion, taking Moody's work to a whole new level. Tracking the salvation responses of his campaigns would have been an insurmountable undertaking, but a very conservative estimate would be in the hundreds of thousands.

Yet away from the dramatic crusades, the beautiful fragrance of Christ lingers. Torrey would often speak about this, guiding any listener back to the moment he first caught its bouquet in the pages of his book.

The book was written amid a three-year prayer meeting taking place in the grounds of the Moody Institute. This period of intercession drew those on the ground in an inexplicably supernatural way and would eventually bear fruit in the Welsh and Azusa Street revivals a few years later. Approximately 400 people gathered weekly with bended knees and tear-filled eyes to pray for God to pour out a worldwide revival.

When numbers dwindled after its third year, Torrey continued with an intimate group of friends. There was a sense of expectation that reached many countries around the globe, and when they heard that hundreds of students were petitioning for revival, focus once more centred on Torrey's leadership. It was this that caused him to gather his thoughts in a book intriguingly titled, *How to Pray*.

It seemed to reflect the label he had been given of 'revival prayer expert'. Tales of his work and commitment to revival had filtered around the world, and now many urged him to outline the path for fellow pilgrims. Torrey had rejected the status of 'expert' in the past and had no intention of laying hold of it now.

For years he had explored how to be true to his call, but at the same time had affirmed that he, like everyone else, only saw the truth in part. Yet the lessons he was about to articulate would have significance far beyond the words he penned, shaping his own future steps and opening his senses to the sweet smell of heaven.

Carefully considering his own journey and what he had been taught by his late friend Moody, he focused on the revival partnership of Charles Finney and Father Daniel Nash. It was an interesting story. Many knew how before any visit of Finney, Father Nash would soak the location in intercessory prayer, sometimes unbeknown to Finney.

It was common for this example to be used as a 'how-to' guide for mission work, with students of evangelism seeking out a partner in prayer. Torrey saw the synergy between prayer and the preaching of the Word, and continued to pursue it throughout all his missionary days. Yet he was disturbed by how narrowly this story was defined, as a quick and easy guide for success.

He drew readers back to an element of the story recognised by Finney himself, with the DNA of pilgrims who had gone on before. He quotes Finney:

> And here I must introduce the name of a man, whom I shall have occasion to mention frequently, Mr. Abel Clary. He was the son of a very excellent man, and an elder of the church where I was converted. He was converted in the same revival in which I was. He had been licensed to preach; but his spirit of prayer was such, he was so burdened with the souls of men that he was not able to preach much, his whole time and strength being given to prayer.

> The burden of his soul would frequently be so great that he was unable to stand, and he would writhe and groan in agony. I was well acquainted with him, and knew something of the wonderful spirit of prayer that was upon him. He was a very silent man, as almost all are who have that powerful spirit of prayer . . .

> I knew at the time a considerable number of men who were exercised in the same way. A Deacon P-, of Camden, Oneida county; a Deacon T-, of Rodman, Jefferson county; a Deacon B-, of Adams, in the same county; and this Mr. Clary and many others among the men, and a large number

of women partook of the same spirit, and spent a great part of their time in prayer.

Father Nash, as we called him, which in several of my fields of labour came to me and aided me, was another of those men that had such a powerful spirit of prevailing prayer. This Mr. Clary continued in Rochester as long as I did, and did not leave it until after I had left. He never, that I could learn, appeared in public, but gave himself wholly to prayer (Torrey, 1903).

Torrey reaffirmed Finney's view that the partnership of Word and prayer was more than what could be seen. Whether it was Mr. Clary, the various deacons, or the nameless men and women 'that partook of the same spirit', the collaboration of mission was more than the limited picture seen by the public.

It was a lesson Torrey took to heart in 1902, as he shaped the future crusades of 1903/1904 around the same premise, with trust that God's hand would eventually connect everything, and heartfelt appreciation of the saints tilling the land before, during and after his time. Aware that this tour of the United Kingdom needed more than just his own words, he called on an old student called Charles Alexander, who was saved as a teenager under Moody's ministry.

Alexander would be to Torrey what Sankey was to Moody, a gospel singer who amplified the message in ways that words alone could not achieve. Meeting him in Melbourne, Australia, he noted that a band of people had been praying for revival every week, echoing the meetings at the institute back home. By the time he had heard of this group, they had grown to over 40,000 people in 2,000 home prayer meetings in 50 cities across the country. This only reinforced his belief of the unseen work of the Creator God, as unseen prayer meetings worked in unison with those in Chicago.

As the crusade started its tour around Britain, Alexander met his future wife, Helen, the daughter of the Quaker philanthropist and reformer Richard Cadbury. Their marriage would become a ministry of activism that developed many initiatives, including a project that Torrey had dreamed of himself without ever seeing its full realisation.

They created the 'Pocket Testament League', a convenient way of carrying Scripture coupled with a pledge to read it each day. This venture reached countless people across the globe, regardless of war, social boundaries and political barriers. Through others' actions,

Torrey witnessed the realisation of what once was a dream inspired by his first conversation with Moody, the Bible placed in many hands.

During this tour he also observed how many diverse groups across the country were all praying for the same thing: God's presence to soak the land. Torrey could not fully explain what he saw, nor did all of it accord with his own theology. But he recognised the signposts pointing to God's work, and invested time and energy into linking different groups together. The resulting collaboration between churches, business groups and evangelistic ministries broadened awareness.

It's not coincidental that Torrey's tour touched many of the praying hotspots, or that all were connected to the famous 1904 revival and its expressions throughout the United Kingdom. This beautiful tapestry of lives divinely woven together captured Torrey's heart and influenced his writings. These were more than just words on a page. He lived them out, and saw first-hand how his own journey was woven into a magnificent work of art of which he himself was only but a part.

A tale of two approaches

It was the best of times, it was the worst of times, it was the age of wisdom, it was the age of foolishness, it was the epoch of belief, it was the epoch of incredulity, it was the season of light, it was the season of darkness, it was the spring of hope, it was the winter of despair, we had everything before us, we had nothing before us, we were all going direct to Heaven, we were all going direct the other way – in short, the period was so far like the present period, that some of its noisiest authorities insisted on its being received, for good or for evil, in the superlative degree of comparison only.

(Charles Dickens: *A Tale of Two Cities*)

Victorian England truly saw the best and worst of times. It was a season of light and darkness, as hope and despair danced together. The Industrial Revolution had transformed the country and brought abundant wealth to selected citizens. Yet by the end of the 19th century, this economic force propelled over 80% of its population into the cities.

This revolution went beyond factories and machinery. The attitudes to knowledge, work and craftsmanship were all caught up in the whirlwind of advancement. Position, location, family, income and education, all affected whether one caught the wind into a land flowing with milk and honey, or was taken on a journey of survival, adaptation or eradication.

Although change was gradual, its effects were widespread. A creative swirl of innovation heralded fresh hope, while new divisions caused a tidal wave of fear. What was thought stable was now found to have uncertain footings, as everyone had to re-interpret the 'signs of the times'.

There were both victors and victims, those living in the new city slums and those in the gleaming corridors of power and position. The worldwide praise bestowed upon Victorian England, as it led in the promotion of new mechanisms and practices, also left a bitter after-taste. This Dickensian storyline included many diverse characters, including two families from opposite backgrounds and experiences, yet unified in their expression of compassion.

William Bramwell Booth was born in March 1856, the eldest child of the famous couple William and Catherine Booth, the founders of the Salvation Army. The family was committed to challenging the nation's conscience, by preaching the gospel in word and deed. They believed in a partnership of the spiritual and practical, though their motto of the three 'S's' (Soap, Soup and Salvation), did not go down well with everyone. Even some believers opposed them, but the family pressed on regardless of rejection, misunderstanding or even violence, walking the path of joy and pain ever present for those on a radical pilgrimage.

The Booth's journey of faith went far beyond the glare of public attention. Behind closed doors they faced a scarcity of funds, but they trusted God with a sense of purpose and pride. Bramwell said years later that his mother 'not only patched our clothes, but made us proud of the patches'. They mixed mission with family life, jointly walking out their call, which their children followed sincerely. As one Booth child said,

> My parents did not have to say a word to me about Christianity. I saw it in action (Salvation Army Heritage Centre).

In 1881 Bramwell was appointed Chief of Staff for the Salvation Army, a post he held until his succession as General after his father's death in 1912. Although certain quarters of the Army questioned his leadership in management and communication, the multi-national work was safely guided through the turbulent waters of the First World War.

His latter years saw the fluctuating heights and lows of success and depression. While the Army's work for holistic salvation bore fruit, inner power struggles eventually led to him being voted from his position. These battles cut deep, but Bramwell's commitment to compassion provided a healing balm. His passion for comprehensive change led him to leave the comforts of a church building or cosy living room for the dark ugly gutters of city life. And eventually he found a surprising connection with a man from a different level of society.

Anthony Ashley Cooper was born in April 1801, and following his father's death became the Seventh Earl of Shaftesbury. Educated at Harrow, and then Christ Church, Oxford, he entered Parliament in 1826. Although not the greatest of orators, his family connections and status all groomed him for a distinguished career in government. Yet he took a different route after being exposed to the darker side of the community he served.

His early Parliamentary duties led him to sit on a committee to gather evidence concerning the mistreatment of 'lunatics'. Committed to bringing hidden practices into the open, he spoke of the horrors of such places as the 'Crib Room', a space set aside for incontinent patients. A place, as one observer recalled,

> where there is nothing but wooden cribs or bedsteads, cases in fact, filled with straw and covered with a blanket, in which these unfortunate beings are placed at night, and they sleep most of them naked on the straw, and of course do all their occasions in their crib (Pollock, 1985).

The committee's report also highlighted other practices such as binding hands and feet with chains, limiting food, and harsh washing conditions. The experience forever remained with Shaftesbury, as he remembered 'the sounds that assailed my ear and the sights that shocked my eye'. His determination to tell that story eventually produced a complete reform of the Lunacy Act.

The Earl also stepped outside his comfort zone to investigate employment. Visiting hospitals with harsh working conditions and the lack of safety protection set him on a course of introducing change. He exposed child labour under the guise of apprenticeship and raised the issue of long working hours. The changes of law that resulted transformed many working practices.

Shaftesbury's passion to help those in need was exemplified through his involvement with education. An advertisement in *The Times* newspaper for a teacher for a new movement called 'Ragged Schools' caught his eye. This charitable project provided free education on Sunday and Thursday evenings for thousands of children and adults who were deemed too unkempt for normal schools.

Shaftesbury became chairman of this work, which was previously chronicled in Dickens' writings, including *Oliver Twist*. Providing more than just academic learning, it included the distribution of food and clothing and even lodging. This approach was later picked up by the national school system, with ideas such as free milk and after hour's clubs founded in this learning revolution.

Shaftesbury's efforts were prolific and the impact was great, so it is not surprising that his passion for social reform led to a meeting with the Booth family. The first encounter was through a tea party he held on the 22nd March 1872 in order to bring together a number of mission projects in London. The aim was to encourage, stir up one another and share good practice.

Catherine Booth, who was standing in for her husband, gave a passionate talk about the work of their 'Christian Mission'. But this positive impression was destroyed six years later when Shaftesbury disagreed with the approach of this mission work, criticising the use of such titles as the 'Salvation Army' and 'General' and the needless 'spiritual gymnastics' of their enthusiasm.

The paths of Shaftesbury and the Booth family diverged, but connected again through the issue of child-sex slavery, an issue which both had been working to eradicate for many years. In July 1885, Bramwell Booth partnered with the journalist William Thomas Stead and a reformed prostitute Rebecca Jarrett, to purchase a young child, to prove that the child sex trade was going on in the streets of London.

Stead was not your typical moral champion as he *"broke almost every rule imaginable. An inveterate flirt who was often caught kissing visitors in the editor's office, he spent decades campaigning against sexual immorality. He twisted the truth, invented quotations and doctored pictures. He tried to get the Pope to relocate to London, campaigned for the Boers against the British and even claimed to be in touch with Winston Churchill's dead father"* (Robinson, 2012). Often guilty of arrogance, he declared himself the guardian of morals, believing that the newspaper was the only Bible millions would read, so it must live up to the convicting words of Scripture. In years to come he would help ghost write William Booth's vision for the eradication of poverty, *In Darkest England And The Way Out*, and would lay claim to being the editor that missed the potential of a writer named Arthur Conan Doyle (creator of the famous fictional detective, Sherlock Holmes).

Yet this contradictory character whose famous last recorded words before his death on the Titanic was *"Well, I guess it's nothing serious; I'm going back to my cabin to read"* (ibid, 2012), found a common bond of justice with Booth. Aware of the potential legal consequences of their controversial acts, they purchased a thirteen-year-old girl called Eliza.

Through Stead's newspaper articles entitled *The Maiden Tribute of Modern Babylon*, they revealed this practice. The story shocked the nation to the core, as it revealed the raw reality of life for many children in the slums, and provoked an intense debate. However, the protagonists had to face trial for their questionable actions. Bramwell was acquitted, but Stead, Jarrett and a midwife called Louise Mouret were given jail terms between three to six months.

Meanwhile, Shaftesbury was visiting the offices of the new Prime Minister, Salisbury and the Home Secretary, Cross. He urged them to support the need for reform highlighted by this story. In August, the

Criminal Law Amendment Act 1885 was enacted, raising the age of consent, and providing more protection for the vulnerable.

This truly was a tale of two approaches, as Shaftesbury and Bramwell tackled a common cause in differing ways. Yet an unseen hand was at work and showed the strength of their unity when the time was right.

Thoughts

But in fact God has placed the parts in the body,
every one of them, just as he wanted them to be.

If they were all one part, where would the body be?
As it is, there are many parts, but one body.

(1 Corinthians 12:18-20)

Many years ago, I was given my first trainee managerial post in the company I had just joined. It was to be alongside an elderly man who was admired by many, with a legendary record of success and commitment. It was a chance this young upstart was not going to miss, and one that I assumed would propel me up the promotional ladder. Yet the experience was instead a life lesson that has forever remained in my mind.

My first day was a cocktail of nerves as I checked my tie every few minutes while attempting to appear confident and assured, rehearsing a few lines of thanks that I would give to my respected mentor. Arriving early, I waited outside his door, expecting a throne room of trophies displaying his work ethic and economic knowledge.

Instead, I saw a room with a few pieces of furniture, pictures of those he loved and a number of scattered reports yet to be processed. Our exchange of greetings was like Luca Brasi in *The Godfather*, as he fluffed up his prepared lines during the wedding of Don Corleone's daughter. Thankfully before I could utter, 'may their first child be a masculine child', I was ushered to the chair, signalling that our meeting was about to begin.

Assuming I was to be given some important task or commission, I sat up straight and made it obvious I was giving him my full attention. With a gentle smile that I grew to appreciate over the years, he said that he wanted to give me a piece of advice which I would grow to understand over time.

Pointing to a pin board behind me, he asked, 'What do you see?' On it was a number of different cards, a series of blue, yellow, pink, orange, green and red. 'Now look at me . . . next time you look back, focus on just one colour'. I obeyed, focusing on the colour green, and then diverted my gaze back to him. 'Good, now let's chat about what we have to do over the next month'.

For the next hour, we went through various tasks that needed to be done, while I was still slightly bewildered at the whole card exercise. I assumed that old age had caused him to forget the punch line, or that it was a test of my willingness to obey whatever he asked me to do.

As the meeting concluded and I made my way to the door, he grabbed my shoulder as if he had suddenly remembered something. 'Quickly, look at the board and without counting, what colour has the most cards pinned to it?' At a glance it was clear that there were significantly more green cards. 'Why don't you count them now?' So I did, and there was the same number in each colour! 'That's my advice, young man. Whatever you choose to focus on will become the dominant thing. Remember that when you need to see the bigger picture'.

Over time my mentor's lesson became invaluable, and it comes to mind when I consider the stories of Bramwell and Shaftesbury. Bramwell had to recognise that the system of stature and wealth that he detested was also a tool to access the corridors of power in his time of need. Similarly, Shaftesbury saw that the daring nature of the Salvation Army which he distrusted was the very thing to provoke a national response towards the cause that he for so long had championed. With their minds fixed on their own colours, neither saw eye to eye. But there is value in all the colours of the spectrum.

It is worth noting that the things we focus on are just a part of something far broader. In our pursuit of a higher cause, we may need to be in partnership with those we disagree with. Sometimes unity has a way of expressing itself in creative diversity. Being together doesn't necessarily mean standing in the same place and expressing our actions in identical ways. It is fellowship of a body made up of many parts, one that could be said is 'an offer we just can't refuse'.

Walking towards the same horizon

Bind us together Lord. Bind us together with cords
that cannot be broken.

We are the family of God. We are the promise divine. We are
God's chosen desire. We are the glorious new wine.

(Bob Gillman: *Bind Us Together*)

Fear gripped the gathering crowd. With cries and anxious questions they watched fire engulfing the Houses of Parliament in 1834. In a frenzied circus of activity, some tried to break through the temporary barriers, as calls for help echoed through the sounds of crackling wood and collapsing structures. Others just stood in disbelief, as the symbol of the country's power and stability crumbled before their eyes.

The first call for help went out at 6 pm on the 16th October, relaying the startling news that the building was now ablaze. In a few short hours, flames were taking hold of the site, but the determined work of fire-fighters and a change in wind direction meant that the 'Great Fire' was finally brought under control. The cherished Westminster Hall had survived the inferno along with a few other buildings, but fire had laid ruin to the charred ground.

It transpired that the Clerk of Works and two workmen had disposed of wooden counting devices known as tally sticks by burning them in the furnaces beneath the House of Lords. It was a decision that was soon regretted, as the intense heat caught hold of the wooden panels of the building. The three were blamed for the destruction.

But Her Majesty, Queen Adelaide, echoed the rumours that this was divine retribution for the Representation of the People Act passed a few years earlier. Perhaps this was a sign from God that power should be centred on only a select few.

This eighteen-foot-long document, commonly known as the Great Reform Act of 1832, aimed to balance out the unrepresentative voting system. Up until that moment, only adult men could vote if they had paid certain taxes or owned property worth a minimum of forty shillings. In some cases an MP could be chosen by a small group or powerful conglomerate that was able to become the puppet master.

The reform act attempted to reduce the number of MPs while doubling the number of eligible voting adult males to approximately 650,000 (about 18% of the population). It also highlighted the so called 'rotten boroughs' – areas with a disproportionately small electorate which used bribes, or in current parlance, 'cash for questions'.

Although women and the working class were still ignored, and there was a blatant bias towards status and wealth, the Bill did represent radical and disturbing change - particularly in the eyes of landowners and power brokers. Yet the Bill was just a chapter in a larger book being written in the nation.

The closing period of the eighteenth century saw great turmoil in Europe. The French Revolution struck fear in seats of earthly authority, showing in vivid colour the power of grass-root movements. Its contradictory declaration of freedom delivered through the fearful and violent persecution of the 'Reign of Terror' intensified debate about who should or could hold the keys of power.

Meanwhile, what some would later describe as the 'Methodist Revolution' had swept through the United Kingdom, as the gospel message was combined with peaceful activism. This counter revolt of political and social change continually evolved into diverse forms.

Sir Samuel Romilly was born in 1757. A highly respected legal expert and Member of Parliament, he was one of the first to support Granville Sharp and Thomas Clarkson in the formation of the Society for the Abolition of the Slave Trade. His involvement in this work also connected him to John Wesley and William Wilberforce.

Romilly was also interested in the French Revolution, particularly its focus on legal reform. Despite his 'horror of every kind of innovation', he was committed to see its legal arguments find some footing in his home country. He tirelessly argued for the political rights of all people groups – a pursuit that merged very effectively with the work of the abolition movement.

Romilly tried to safeguard the threatened Habeas Corpus Act, which gave anyone who was being detained by the authorities the right to have their case heard before a court of law. He advocated reform of the criminal justice system, believing that it should be biased towards political liberty and human rights, though he questioned universal suffrage, maintaining that the right to vote required educated debate and political understanding. His passion for protecting values through the statute books made a lasting impact on society, despite his suicide in 1818 after the death of his beloved wife.

Robert Raikes, born in 1736, was famed for his work with the Sunday School movement. He was also a campaigner for prison reform and social care for families of prisoners. Observing how travelling preachers like George Whitefield were using their sermons to address injustice, he creatively used the newspaper, the *Gloucester Journal* to promote the cause of social reform.

Encouraged by the development of localised education springing up from faith groups such as the Methodists, Raikes also started to effectively make use of the one day that working children had off from their labours: Sunday. Focusing on the schoolroom and regular home visits, his work gathered weight in the movement for social reform. He believed that the growing unrest and violence in Europe could be prevented by a national programme teaching Biblical morals. Raikes' movement promoted education to over a quarter of the nation's children, and provoked government recognition of a child's right to education.

Sarah Trimmer was born in 1741. Daughter of a respected artist, she was acquainted with such characters as the painter and social commentator William Hogarth, and the famed writer and producer of the *Dictionary of the English Language*, Dr. Samuel Johnson. As they discussed developing education as a means of progression for society, she became closely associated with the Sunday school movement started by Robert Raikes. Although Trimmer's views differed from Raikes', specifically in her conviction that education for the poor must reinforce their position in the hierarchy of manual labour, she was committed to ensuring that all people, regardless of status, be given tools for learning.

Suspicious of imaginative works such as fairy-tales, Trimmer produced and published a series of instructive and moral books for children to read which mixed nature, history and Scripture lessons. Her encouragement of learning and promotion of equality for women authors lived on beyond her sometimes dated and restrictive methods, and was picked up by the writers of a radical and respected publication, the *Edinburgh Review*. This connection brought opportunities to widen the debate about reform and social responsibility within the Gospel message.

Hannah More was born in 1745. As a member of a group of influential social reformers called the 'Clapham Sect' and friend of Dr. Samuel Johnson, William Wilberforce, Granville Sharpe and John Newton, discussion of reform and activism were always close at hand. Like Sarah Trimmer, More had firm beliefs about a strict social hierarchy, saying, 'Beautiful is the order of society when each according to his place pays willing honour to his superiors . . . Satisfied with his own place', yet put a high value on the individual.

Best known as a playwright, teacher and philanthropist, Hannah regularly partnered literature and business with the reform agenda. By ensuring that the publication of her poem 'Slavery' coincided with the first debate in parliament on the issues of the slave trade, she broadened the public discourse. Through her *Village Politics* writings, she countered the individualistic approach of the French Revolution by speaking out for Biblical morals and social responsibility.

Hannah never avoided facing political debate head on. Her creative approach to the *Cheap Repository Tracts*, an affordable publication that focused on moral and social issues, complemented her controversial writings about the injustice of giving women a second-rate education. She helped establish a number of schools within her local area, all of which supported the Sunday school movement, and furthered exposure of the work in the social circles she regularly moved in.

Revd. Sidney Smith was born in 1771, and is noted as one of the founders of the *Edinburgh Review* in 1802. Also known as the *Critical Journal*, this quarterly publication critiqued Parliament and examined social issues at a time when doing such a thing could be deemed treason. Initially writing under pseudonyms, the writers creatively promoted reformist views on social liberty, abolition of the slave trade and the encouragement of local activism.

Smith's fame spread across the sea to Abraham Lincoln. The sixteenth President of the United States of America often used his carefully crafted, witty phrases as he articulated reformist ideals.

Another reformer was the young lawyer and journalist Henry Brougham. His interest in the advancement of learning and the cause of anti-slavery eventually led him to pursue a seat in Parliament. Through the help of William Wilberforce, he won one of the 'rotten boroughs' in 1810, and immediately used his parliamentary position to legislate against the trade in human beings. He also addressed the inequality of property ownership between men and women, while promoting the rights of agricultural workers.

Brougham also fought for change in the House itself, particularly of inequities in the voting system and the 'rotten boroughs' system that had got him into Parliament in the first place, and eventually welcomed the *Representation of the People Act* in 1832.

William Cobbett was born in 1763. Originally a soldier in the British Army, he spoke out against the harsh conditions and corrupt practices he had observed in a controversial article called *The Soldiers' Friend* in 1792. He fled to France to avoid prosecution, but the revolution that was sweeping the country meant that he had to once again flee, this time to America.

The stir his writings created eventually brought a lawsuit against him, so he returned to England. Controversy continued with his *Political Register*, a pioneering weekly publication that recorded the Parliamentary discourse when such debates were forbidden to be heard by the pubic. By reducing the cost, he made sure that it would reach the working class.

After failing four times to win a parliamentary seat, he finally became MP for Oldham in the same year as the reform act of 1832. Never shying away from a fight, he used his few short years in Parliament before his death in 1835, to expose some of the corrupt laws that oppressed the poor and marginalised.

The writings of the *Political Register*, in particular those of Francis Burdett, the son-in-law of the famous banking family, Coutts, inspired Sir Samuel Romilly's passion for law reform. Although Romilly's dreams were never fulfilled due to his untimely death, it was yet another connecting thread in the movement.

In the chorus of political activism across the land these are just a few names, each performer bringing their own tone of faith. From solos to mass choirs of participation, individual vision found a home in a collective partnership. Some enthusiastically collaborated, while others remained ignorant of the wider picture. Yet together they formed an ensemble that built on the work of pilgrims of faith from a century earlier. These new harmonies of compassion rang out the divine song of social reform.

Thoughts

> Can you sense the Creator, world? Seek Him above the starry canopy. Above the states He must dwell. Be embraced, millions.

> This kiss for all the world. Brother, above the starry canopy, A loving Father must dwell.

> (Ludwig van Beethoven: *Ode to Joy*, adapted from Friedrich Schiller's poem *An die Freude*)

On the top floor of the National Portrait Gallery in London, is Room 20. It houses a collection of portraits depicting *The Road to Reform*, representing reformers in both paintings and sculpture. The hushed room lays out in one pictorial oeuvre a series of individual lives: writers, politicians, housewives and teachers, all with differing agendas and expressions of faith, but who have all walked the same path to reform.

The centrepiece and largest image of them all is the painting of the House of Commons by Sir George Hayter, commemorating the passing of the 1832 Reform Act. The scene depicts this celebrated moment of history as prominent figures in both the Whig and Tory camps take their place in unified dignity. This masterpiece provides a finale like the last movement in Beethoven's ninth Symphony, an *Ode to Joy* echoing in the corridors of the famous British gallery. Each time I gaze on it, it takes me back to the moment in history's timeline linking other stories and events.

Completeness is defined not as a final and irrevocable conclusion, but as having 'all the necessary or appropriate parts'. It invites us to re-imagine what it means to be complete in a weaving dance of individual steps.

Do we consider ourselves unimportant in the broad scheme of things? On the other hand, do we arrogantly believe that this vast world revolves around our own dreams and thoughts? Or do we fall on our knees in adoration of a God who invites us to participate in a symphony that he has beautifully orchestrated? Through the distinctive callings each one of us has, our fingerprints become part of his handprint in the world.

A man in between

When you find a spark of grace in the heart,
kneel down and blow it into a flame.

(Charles Haddon Spurgeon: September 17th *Morning
and Evening Readings*)

In the crispness of the winter air, two funerals took place: one in
December 1691, the other in November 1770. Despite the different
dates and locations, the two memorials shared a common bond that
provided a warm blanket for the mourners and fellow pilgrims of faith.

The first funeral was of a man called Richard Baxter. Born in 1615,
he had a nomadic existence in his early childhood, travelling between
his parents' and grandparents' home, due to the gambling and inherited
debts of his father. Although everyone attempted to make those times
fun for 'little Baxter', financial pressure from debt collectors gave a
sense of uncertainty to each day.

This was dramatically transformed when his father found salvation
through the 'bare reading of the Scriptures in private'. What followed
was an intense redirection of his father's life, as he shunned the
escapism of gambling and instead focused his attention on repaying
his debts. This transformation brought Baxter back home to enjoy
family life, now an active believer.

Although his early education was limited, Baxter's teenage years
were surrounded by an exciting atmosphere of political and faith-led
debate. His family regularly held meetings for teachers, including
Anglican clergy, non-conformists and potential dissenters, exploring
ideologies to do with justice and the expression of belief. Years before
the Civil War and the rise of Oliver Cromwell, Baxter was already being
exposed to the varied arguments that were brewing.

During the turmoil of the Civil War, Baxter became the curate for
Kidderminster in 1641. He had a passion for the lost, preaching as 'a
dying man to dying men', a fervency that was also embodied in his
prayers. He was often seen combining his parish duties with prayer,
intensely focused on bringing the needs of those around him into the
loving embrace of God.

Some tried to focus the political debate on royalty and the
distribution of wealth, but Baxter recognised that this was something
far more complex – it was about faith and about injustice. Meanwhile,

traditional ways of living and working were becoming marginalised, through what seemed an oppressive and arrogant social agenda.

Despite the complexity of issues a common voice was beginning to rise. Baxter trod carefully, aware of the dangers of trying to funnel divergent voices through one mouthpiece, but also acknowledging the message being delivered so succinctly through the Parliamentary Army. He offered his services as a garrison chaplain, but as he toured the battlefields, he became troubled by the growing prejudice of the soldiers in its regiments.

This exposure strengthened Baxter's belief that such intolerance is alien to the Christian walk. His unease eventually led to a sermon that he delivered to Cromwell after his victory, focusing on encouraging freedom of thought and faith in the country, as well as respecting royalty. He repeated this message during Cromwell's *'Protectorship'* reign and the later restoration of the monarchy, and found himself continually in the middle of conflicting parties.

Continued debates raged in the country, with opposing parties of thought concerning church versus state. The opposing religious factions each blamed the other for causing a utopia to be lost before it was truly gained. Even during the Savoy Conference, established to seek reconciliation in the fractured church after the return of Charles II, Baxter had to build bridges between enemy camps. It hadn't escaped the notice of royalty that many who professed faith were also part of the Parliamentary Army, so there was fear of retaliation.

To safeguard the established church as well as their own positions, the conference developed the Clarendon Code – legislation demanding that all municipal officials be part of the Anglican Communion and making use of the *Book of the Common Prayer* compulsory. It also required all to swear an oath of allegiance to the king, forbade people from gathering for worship that was not state authorised, and restricted non-conformist ministers from preaching or teaching in schools.

Baxter fought vehemently to change the code, yet failed. His worst fear had come true, as a line was drawn between 'us' and 'them' within the faith, which would surely lead to bloodshed and the rejection of *'one body but many parts'*. Although he continued to argue for change, his pious stance respected both lines of thought and he worked actively for unity. In these early days there was still hope, but that was soon dashed. He made a stand that would cost him dearly, when he was offered the role of Bishop and turned it down.

The years that followed saw persecution, oppression, confiscation of his books and possessions, criminal charges for writing a paraphrase of the New Testament, and imprisonment for holding a Conventicle (unofficial worship meeting). Through it all he remained steadfast, committed to finding a harmonious way between the diverse expressions of faith. Despite the pain, Baxter continued with his cause, expressing his thoughts through whatever means he could find.

Whilst his theology could be sometimes questioned, his passion to draw out the divine gems in every person's expression of faith could never be doubted. The passing of the Toleration Act in 1689 gave him a couple of peaceful years before his death in 1691.

In his last moments, a friend reminded him of the impact his writing had upon the country. He simply replied, 'I was but a pen in God's hand, and what praise is due a pen?' (Buck, 1822).

On a winter's day in December 1691, he was buried in the sight of established clergymen, dissenters and non-conformists. These opposing groups had battled in recent years, yet that day they gathered together around the grave of a man who had worked tirelessly to persuade them to stand side by side.

The second funeral was also on a winter's day: a Sunday in November 1770. An aged man in his late sixties stood by the grave of his departed dear friend. Over the years they had had many debates about Calvinist and Arminian theology. Their disagreement over such issues as conditional or unconditional election, general or limited atonement, and the believer's responsibility in salvation, had caused tension. Sometimes their warm embraces were followed by a cold shoulder, but they knew that one day they would embrace in their eternal home.

They had strong memories of moments in time like their youth in Oxford as they toiled together in a club to encourage members in the practice of prayer, the study of Scripture, the examination of the heart and charitable service to the poor. They were mocked for their methodical code of practice shaped from the reading of *Rules of Holy Living* by Bishop Taylor. Yet it was a treasured time for both of them, which laid a foundation for daring acts of pilgrimage.

Both shared a passion to evangelise the nations for Christ, to face injustice head on and to speak out against sinful living. They were determined not to shy away from opposition but to be brave enough to speak up for truth, even if it cost them dearly. And despite their differing opinions on social issues such as slavery, they travelled the nation in unison. Their journey of sermons and social action was part of a wider revolution that rocked the country and beyond.

The man standing by his friend's grave was John Wesley. His own work had grown rapidly alongside his departed companion, George

Whitefield, as the gospel message had spread to society with almost unimaginable success. This radical movement of lay preachers, localised chapels and outdoor preaching had been greatly inspired by Whitefield's approach to working the mission field. Their paths had ventured into the halls of power, the care for the poor, an educational movement and the independence of America.

There had been frustrations about their conflicting sermons and occasionally opposing actions. Yet regardless of their differences, the bond of friendship was honoured once again as Wesley gave the closing sermon.

> What an honour it pleased God to put upon His faithful servant, by allowing to declare His ever lasting Gospel in so many various countries, to such numbers of people, and with so great an effect on so many of their precious souls. Have we read or heard of any person since the apostles, who testified the Gospel of grace? . . . Have we read or heard any person, who called so many thousands, so many myriads of sinners to repentance? Above all, have we read or heard of any, who has been a blessed instrument in the hand of God, of bringing so many sinners from darkness to light, and from the power of Satan unto God? (Wesley, 1831).

As a dear life was celebrated, it was also a time of painful loss. Whatever theological differences, they were never separate from the ultimate cause. Their opinions often varied and they may have stumbled in working out their partnership, but they both cherished the author Richard Baxter, whose written works were mentioned by both with deep affection. How appropriate that this seventieth-century servant of Christ somehow shared in a funeral that represented opposing theologies standing together as one.

Thoughts

> Trusting as the moments fly, trusting as the days go by.
> Trusting Him whatever befall, trusting Jesus that is all.
>
> (Ira D. Sankey: *Trusting Jesus – Sacred Songs and Solos with Standard Hymns*)

The connection between an author and his or her pen is an intimate one as ideas are shaped on a page. There must be a harmony of weight, feel, and balance in the hand. The interaction of the creator and the created brings forth the calligraphy of style and graceful expression.

This is captured in Baxter's statement, 'I was but a pen in God's hand, and what praise is due a pen?' (Buck, 1822). This was his humble response to human praise of his efforts. He devoted his life to unifying Christians and his faithful work endured beyond his years in two men of God who are heroes of our faith.

Wesley and Whitefield struggled with each other, their disagreements many times leading them to walk separate paths. But something drew them back, a heartbeat that could not be easily silenced. Forgotten details of their writings reveal the common figure of Richard Baxter, and his challenge to rigorously pursue unity in the body of Christ.

The wealth of the believer is not in earthly riches, but in the love of Christ. Placing ourselves in the hand of our Creator is an act of worshipful trust given to the Author who crafts his dreams on the pages of our lives. He takes us, like a pen that is perfectly weighted, to create a masterpiece that will outlive us.

When our heart grasps the wonder of this, the words 'what praise is due a pen?' take on a new realm of meaning. The answer to its question echoes throughout time. The praise is in the creation from the Creator's hand.

Note 'A'
Precious weakness

Introduction: In love's service

Today, the major events of Jesus' life are marked on calendars around the world – Christmas, Good Friday, and Easter. Of the three, however, only the middle one, the crucifixion, took place in the open for all the world to see. At the moment when God seemed downright helpless, the cameras of history were rolling.

(Philip Yancey: *Disappointment with God*)

You have searched me, Lord, and you know me...

You perceive my thoughts from afar...

Before a word is on my tongue, you, Lord, know it completely.

In David's sacred song, Psalm 139, he depicts what it is to be human. Alongside a staggering description of the omnipresence of God is an image of humanity at many levels, both exposed and hidden. Words spoken in public and quiet thoughts that no one could hear, prominent acts as well as the mundane motions of getting up out of bed; our entire life is captured in the gaze of the Creator. It reassures us that God knows our true being.

The well-known quotation, 'You should never meet your heroes, as they will disappoint you', is a premise equally flawed and insightful, as a conversation or Internet search will reveal stories both of joy and despair.

We may be surprised by the rebellious, hotel room smashing rock star who sits next to a young truant, quoting from the philosopher Alain Badiou before lecturing him on the discipline of education. On the other hand, an actor who radiates looks and intelligence on screen while fighting espionage may disappoint on both counts when seen off-camera. The list of stories can go on, some painful, some funny, and some reassuring. Yet all of them hint that the idealised images we construct of those we look up to may not capture all the nuances of their whole being.

This also is true of revival. I love to tell the story of how God's divine power blanketed a community, anointing individuals so that their servant-hearted acts demonstrated heaven's love to those in need. Such heroes become a luminous beacon and inspiration. Some are famous role models, engraved in history, while others are hidden from public sight; just a few appear in this book.

These heroic figures are cherished down the generations, but their powerful exploits can seem dauntingly out of reach by those who feel untouched by destiny's hand. Our admiring re-telling of their stories can remove any jagged edges from the image. Yet their close companions on the journey can tell another story: one that portrays these living stones in a more natural form. This is true of three people in my personal hall of fame: George Whitefield, William Booth and Aimee Semple-McPherson.

Whitefield's daring preaching was a cornerstone of the Great Awakening and his name is rightly praised in revival narratives. Yet it seems that his message was compromised on the question of 'salvation for all', even though he hinted at it through his altar calls. His passion for the value of each life was at odds with the fact that he held slaves, even though he is reported to have treated them with the highest of respect.

Booth was one of the founders of the Salvation Army, a movement which had a great impact on society. But he struggled with the balance of work and home life. While flooding the back streets of the cities with his compassion and determination, his relationship with his own family varied. Some of his children felt the warm embrace of his respect, but others felt the harsh rejection of his stubbornness.

Semple-McPherson's pioneering communication of the gospel message made Hollywood innovators like Charlie Chaplin stand up and take notice. She was the first woman to drive across America coast to coast, spreading the Good News in a trailblazing way. Her commitment to minister to the sick meant many sacrificial moments behind closed doors. Yet she could also be very demanding, seeking public attention and money like that of a movie star.

It could be tempting to lay bare each person's life, intently critiquing every action and exposing their darker sides. Yet we see these contradictions in our own lives: wearing a sweatshop garment while we look for Fair Trade groceries, or wanting to boast of our good deeds, forgetting that our left hand should not know what our right hand is doing.

As we tell stories we may rightly avoid the ugly blemishes that detract from the beauty we want others to see. Rough edges can cut deep, indeed be a safety hazard. Yet when seen through a different lens, a more comprehensive story unfolds that redefines what it is to be perfect.

The pool of Bethesda was a well-known gathering place in Biblical times. This oasis of healing had two conflicting local definitions. For some, it was known as a place of shame, a pitiful display of desperation from those declared as outcasts. Yet to those who needed its healing waters the most, it was a 'house of mercy', welcoming them to a restorative feast laid out on its table.

One man had sat by the pool for 38 years and faced the deep disappointment of failed attempts to reach the waters when they were miraculously stirred. His hope for change was to be answered by a stranger, who asked whether he wanted to get well. The man expected to be assisted towards the pool, but instead heard the words, *'Get up. Pick up your mat and walk.'* This was contrary to his expectations, but his trusting response led to the fulfilment of his long held dream.

One re-telling of this story is intriguing. In 1928 Thornton Wilder told of a physician who keeps coming to the pool of miracles, hoping to be healed from his melancholy. As the water begins to stir, signalling to all surrounding its banks that the time for a miracle has arrived, an angel repeatedly blocks his way, saying, 'This moment is not for you.' Eventually the physician asks why he is being continually prevented from being healed. The angel responds,

> Without your wound, where would your power be? It is your very sadness that makes your low voice tremble into the hearts of men. The very angels themselves cannot

persuade the wretched and blundering children on earth as can one human being broken on the wheels of living. In love's service only the wounded soldiers can serve. Draw back (Wilder, 1928).

The image of lives broken on the wheels of living is not comfortable, but the Master Craftsman knew all along that perfection is truly perfected in the bosom of imperfection. We accept that we are weak before God, but when it comes to our mistakes, shortcomings and character issues, they seem out of place amid such glorious displays of Heaven's power. Yet there is a fine line between the inner tears of a pilgrim and the arrogant smile of a stubborn self-ruler.

One walks with a limp, the other a self-important stroll. One embraces the cross, painfully carrying its splinters, and the other forcefully slams clenched fists of pompous grandeur on a table for attention. In these stark differences we detect the beauty of a broken life. As we serve in love the One true love, there is an authenticity to our vulnerability that no miraculous sign could ever copy.

The story of Brainerd

They were so engrossed with gazing upon the face of God that
they spent scarce a moment looking at themselves. They were
suspended in that sweet paradox of spiritual awareness where they
knew that they were clean through the blood of the Lamb and yet
felt that they deserved only death and hell as their reward. This
feeling is strong in the writings of Paul and is found also in almost all
devotional books and among the greatest and most loved hymns.

(AW Tozer: *Keys to a Deeper Life*)

The life of David Brainerd in the early eighteenth century certainly reads
as an exciting and heart captivating story line. Orphaned at the age of
fourteen, he inherited a farm at nineteen and went to Yale University
when he was twenty. His university years exposed him to revival figures
such as George Whitefield, Gilbert Tennent and Jonathan Edwards.
These visiting preachers encouraged students not to accept the 'norm'
but to ask the questions that matter, even when it brought discomfort.

They modelled a passionate pursuit of spiritual and social awakening,
to lay hold of a heavenly calling that is to be worked out with sober
and dedicated purpose. These men practiced what they preached as
they sought creative ways of communicating the Gospel message
while facing up to the moral issues of the day. As they spoke the truth
with firm inner conviction, their listeners, including the young Brainerd,
could not escape the sharp two-edged sword of the Spirit.

These preachers were the emerging streams of the First Great
Awakening, a revival that swept across America with the message of
personal salvation and moral responsibility. Followers were nicknamed
'new lights', while those who questioned such developments were
called 'old lights'. Brainerd's enthusiasm for this new direction, along
with his tendency to question established authority, led to him being
expelled from Yale. This was a devastating development, and not just
because under Connecticut law the only way to become a minister
was to graduate from selected universities.

A few years earlier, an elderly man by the name of Mr. Fiske had
spent much time before he died investing his thoughts and insights
into Brainerd's life. He pointed to the wisdom of those who walked
faithfully with their Saviour through joy and sorrow, and told him to
continue in devotion, passionately devouring the Bible whenever he
could. This friendship challenged Brainerd to fix his eyes on the inner

call and not to be distracted by side issues, and he chose to follow the call to ministry.

Now that call to become a minister seemed to be smashed, and a sense of having failed his dearly departed friend lay heavy on his heart. But a request came to preach at one of the meetings of a local gathering of believers, and Brainerd swung from bitter discouragement to passionate excitement, taking hold of the opportunity with committed vigour. As he crafted sermons he started a hopeful campaign to get reinstated at the university. Yet, once again he was grievously disappointed when his request was refused, and his cries towards God took on a heavier tone of distress.

During this time a burden started to come on his heart for the unchurched natives, and with the encouragement of his 'new lights' friends, he saw the Wild West as his new parish. For the next few years of his short life, Brainerd travelled to the Native American tribes, bringing the message of Christ as well as practical work of education and justice.

Stories of spiritual and physical salvation filtered to the various communities of the Native Americans about Brainerd's work. He became a champion of their traditions and way of life, fighting the ideas of visitors in their land.

Brainerd's pioneering work was cut short by his failing health. While he lay in bed being nursed in the home of Jonathan Edwards the famous revivalist, Edwards' daughter Jerusha captured his last days in writing. Sadly, Jerusha who had cared so lovingly for this dying missionary, died herself a year later from the same illness. But the journey of Brainerd lives on through the pages of his diary that was compiled into print by his friend and revival teacher, Edwards.

Brainerd was a young man who was committed to a cause, influenced by the wave of revival that was sweeping across the country. He was an ambassador for the living faith, combining the gospel with practical acts and standing up for those who were ignored.

His diary reports countless days in prayer, as a role model for future missionaries. He faced trials and troubles, yet continued at the coalface until his health finally failed him. Even then, he pressed on with his cause, following Fiske's advice to disregard pain and his approaching death.

Yet Brainerd was also a man who questioned himself. His diary records not only words of hope and great achievements, but his despondency over personal failures and the trials he endured. Despite seeing miracles in the tribes and being faithfully committed to his missionary journey, this man of God fell headlong into moments of despair.

Jonathan Edwards honoured this complex mix of faith and sorrow when he wrote of his friend,

> how great and long continued his desires for the spiritual good . . . how he prayed, laboured, and wrestled, and how much he denied himself, and suffered, to this end. After all Mr Brainerd's agonising in prayer, and travailing in birth, for the conversion of Indians, and all the interchanges of his raised hopes and expectations, and then disappointments and discouragements; and after waiting in a way of persevering prayer, labour, and suffering, as it were through a long night; at length the day dawns. Weeping continues for a night, but joy comes in the morning (Edwards, 2007).

Brainerd's life was like a roller-coaster ride, one minute up, then a deep drop down. It may seem uncharacteristic of a revival hero, but after his death, his diary became a classic of the mission field. Its raw words revealed the vulnerable heart of a man who wanted to love God and people, and the reality that our path is not always paved with gleaming stones of success.

Brainerd's honest narrative encouraged future missionaries to speak the truth of their feelings about both their highs and lows. Despite pain and tears, Brainerd reflected the wisdom of his old friend Mr. Fiske, that God's truth is found in an authentic walk of faith which can only be experienced through the pilgrimage we call life.

Thoughts

> And I wake up in the night and feel the dark. It's so hot inside my soul I swear there must be blisters on my heart. So hold me Jesus, 'cause I'm shaking like a leaf. You have been King of my glory, won't you be my Prince of Peace.

> (Rich Mullins: *Hold Me Jesus*)

It was only a few days in the Hebrew calendar, but packed with vivid memories. There were wonderful demonstrations of healing, meals of friendship and laughter, vulnerable moments where their leader washed their feet, and then that moment that left the disciples fearful about the future.

They were already struggling to balance Jesus' agenda with their expectation of salvation from their oppressors. His words about denial and death dashed their fragile hopes, and left them confused about him going to a place that they presently couldn't follow. They were frightened about his prophecy that they would be scattered and hunted down in a world that would hate and persecute them. The heights and lows of these days ended with more questions than satisfactory answers.

Imagine having given up everything to follow a person you placed great trust in. He continually spoke about freedom and redemption, which must surely apply to the occupying army who demanded unfair taxes. Despite his refusal to raise an army, somehow you thought there must be something up his sleeve. Then the bombshell dropped – he would go to a place that no one can follow him to. Moreover, his followers would be hated and despised, forever hunted down.

To be honest, I think that would knock me down. My emotions would run high, with anger, disappointment, and fear, but most of all I would probably want answers that would give me some hope, or at least give meaning to the sacrifices I had already made. I am ashamed to say that words about someone else coming, a Counsellor who would guide me to the truth, probably wouldn't have helped. I would not be looking for another mysterious being when I wanted clarity.

Yet entwined in such an uncertain time, the words are heard

> *Peace, I leave with you; My peace I give you. I do not give to you as the world gives. Do not let your hearts be troubled and do not be afraid.* (John 14:27).

Peace does not always explain the situations we are in. Peace does not always negate the reality of the challenges that are faced. It does not answer all the questions, or stop tears from flowing down our cheeks. But it does reassure us that we are not alone in our decisions and uncertainties. That we travel with the One that truly and forever loves us.

This is why I find the life of David Brainerd so encouraging. In such a short life he achieved so much, travelling the peaks of the spiritual life but also the dark valleys of pain. Hope mingled with disappointment and fear. He sang thankful praise but also cried out in fear that he would never attain such heights ever again. He is not a typical heroic figure, but perhaps he is one of the most real. One who could say,

> Sometimes my life just don't make sense at all. When the mountains look so big, and my faith just seems too small. So hold me Jesus, 'cause I'm shaking like a leaf. You have been King of my glory. Won't You be my Prince of Peace? (Rich Mullins: *Hold Me Jesus*)

Returned a failure

In the evening I went very unwillingly to a society in Aldersgate
Street, where one was reading Luther's preface to the Epistle
to the Romans. About a quarter before nine, while he was
describing the change which God works in the heart through
faith in Christ, I felt my heart strangely warmed. I felt I did
trust in Christ, Christ alone, for salvation; and an assurance was
given me that He had taken away my sins, even mine,
and saved me from the law of sin and death.

(John Wesley's *Journal* entry May 24, 1738)

Much has been written about the life of John Wesley. Many words
have covered his early years at Oxford, and the friendships that shaped
his future, his pursuit of a life that bucked the trend of compromised
living in religious and secular society, the missionary trip to America and
the Moravian travelling companions who deepened his understanding
of salvation, then his return to the United Kingdom, preaching the
Gospel message with forceful energy up and down the nation.

We marvel at Wesley's determination to fight for the abolition of
slavery, and his commitment to unity even when others encouraged
separation, his establishment of local societies for development of
young Christians, and communication of the Gospel in ways that all could
understand. His life-story continues to provide deep encouragement
for many, regardless of denomination – a legacy of his work that remains
despite his death over two hundred years ago.

These famous actions and leaps of faith can so easily create an
intimidating illusion that he was a man of God who lived from victory
to victory, whose character shone so brightly that no one else could
attain such heights. But the life of John Wesley was not perfect. He
struggled with the same temptations, character flaws and storms of
emotions that we all battle with today. He had days of success, and
days when his stubbornness and anger got the best of him, even
during the famous years that surrounded his Moravian experience and
the well known words, 'my heart was strangely warmed'.

That journal entry of May 1738 followed a painful journey that led
back to his Oxford years and a very old red notebook that he
treasured. This old notebook originally belonged to his grandfather,
John Westley, a Puritan preacher who stood up for his beliefs, refusing

to use *The Book of Common Prayer* that was then mandatory. Due to that stance, he received a short prison sentence and lost his income.

Even in those uncertain times, Westley and his wife continued steadfast within their beliefs, and their journey was recorded in that notebook. When that notebook passed down to the young John Wesley, his mother encouraged him to use it for his own self-examination. *(As he used a short hand code for a more private, honest record of his thoughts, his writings have always been hard to fully decipher)*.

Spurred by his reading of George Stanhope's The Christian's Pattern, a paraphrase of Thomas á Kempis' work *The Imitation of Christ*, Wesley started to explore his own ideas of Christian living. At first, the *Imitation* annoyed him. He often complained that he couldn't believe 'that when God sent us into the world, he had irreversibly decreed that we should be perpetually miserable in it . . . That all mirth is vain and useless, if not sinful' (Wesley, 1872). These questions continued as he pursued the passionate call burning within him, with a force that combated the spiritual apathy around him.

Wesley did eventually find some comfort in the words of Kempis and Stanhope. He wrote,

> I began to see that true religion was seated in the heart, and that God's law extended to all our thoughts as well as words and actions (ibid, 1872).

Like a craftsman, he started to mould and reshape his thoughts into a strict code of living, motivated by a desire for radical change. Although he was still unsure about his own salvation, his notebook reveals the sense of pride and self-confidence he had in his own holiness and intellect. His mother even expressed concern about his attitude, saying,

> One act of self-denial is more grateful to your Master than the performance of many duties, as it is an undeniable instance of the love we bear Him (Pollock, 1989).

In October 1735, Wesley, along with his brother Charles, Benjamin Ingham and Charles Delamotte, set sail for the United States of America. His mind was fixed on the idea of being a missionary but he added:

> my chief motive, to which all the rest are subordinate, is the hope of saving my own soul. I hope to learn the true sense of the Gospel of Christ by preaching it to the heathens (Wesley, 1872).

His time in the state of Georgia was not the easiest. Wesley's sermons based on his strict codes of practice caused friction with the settlers.

He preached that frequent religious activities were the demonstration of true Christianity, while his congregation were already struggling with the burdens of work and limited time. Even though some of the town folk tried to reason with him about his lack of awareness of their everyday life, Wesley continued determinedly on his course.

There he met a young 17-year-old girl called Sophia Hopkey, which soon developed into a friendship. Trying to reconcile his own rule 'to have no intimacy with any woman in America' with the subtle hints from Sophia's aunt that she would make a good housewife, the two of them grew in their admiration for each other. His code was pushed to one side when after prayers and conversations, he took her by the hand and 'before we parted I kissed her. And from this time, I fear there was a mixture in my intention, though I was not soon sensible of it' (Pollock, 1989).

In the following months, tensions in the community started to rise up; one lady even threatened to shoot him before setting on him with a pair of scissors because she felt that he had slandered her family. Regardless, he continued, even writing to his friend George Whitefield, asking him to come and join him. But it was the developing story with Sophia that brought the troubles to a head.

The young woman was now engaged to another man, but Wesley still believed that she had romantic feelings for him. Recognising that 'I cannot take fire into my bosom and not be burnt', he decided that he would not consider marriage until he had finished his missionary work among the Indians. However, less than a month later, he returned to the town to find Sophia married to another man.

At first he was able to keep friendship with the new married couple, but soon heard a rumour that this young girl had purposely flirted with him. In his annoyance and shame, he sought to excommunicate her from the church. This angered her husband, who then sued Wesley for defamation of character, and the growing dispute split the community in two.

Eventually Wesley gave notice of his departure from the colony, but Sophia's husband wanted Wesley to stay and answer his financial claim. When the court granted 'refusal of leave', Wesley resorted to escaping from the colony after evening prayers on the 2nd of December 1737, accompanied by three other men, all of questionable repute.

Wesley returned to England as a failed missionary, confused and shamed. Given the opportunity to preach in London after his disappointing mission report to the trustees, he provoked further concern when he dispensed with his wig and dared to preach without notes and showing his long hair. Although this behaviour might seem reasonable, his comments and writings suggested that he relished the opportunity of causing an offence.

Yet in the midst of this inner turmoil, Wesley's paths crossed again with the Moravians on the 7th February, which he described as 'a day much to be remembered'. His conversations with Peter Bohler in Latin (as the German had not learnt English yet), and their travels across England eventually led to the famous meeting in Aldersgate Street and the strangely warmed heart. The following year, Wesley also discovered a revolutionary new form of preaching in the open air after an invitation from his friend George Whitefield.

Although his stubborn nature emerged time and again, the sharp arrow of conviction propelled Wesley forward. His passion-filled walk was perfectly summed up in his obituary in *The Gentleman's Magazine*:

> The great point in which his name and mission will be honoured is this; he directed his labours towards those who had no instructor, to the highways and hedges; to the miners in Cornwall and the colliers in Kingswood . . . By the humane and active endeavours of him and his brother Charles, a sense of decency, morals, and religion was introduced . . . (ibid, 1989).

Thoughts

> Come carry me now. I'm crying out, for someone
> I cannot see. Come carry me now, I'm crying.
>
> How I long to be broken. How I want to be near you.
> How my heart skips beats when your love accepts me as I am.
>
> (The Glorious Unseen: *Burn in Me*)

A journal is a precious record of a person's emotions and thoughts. For some it is a rigid chronicle of events to prompt the memory in years to come. Others use it to download thoughts and feelings of each day. Its pages can be neatly constructed or a frenzied scribble, the penmanship in careful calligraphy or coded shorthand.

The diary of John Wesley details how sermons, codes of living and social action rippled through communities. The effects are still treasured today, but it's the old red notebook passed down from his pioneering grandfather that draws our attention to the complex journey that we all travel. It details a man who humbly yearned for internal change, but also found refuge in proud self-belief, a man who passionately cared for people, yet resorted to stubbornness when facing disagreement and perceived wrongdoing. It is an honest portrayal of each step of a pilgrimage of faith.

We all have a notebook of life, which invites us to be truthful in the words we inscribe on its page. The folios of our days record our hopes and dreams, our fears and doubts. The journal of our successes and failures transcribe our cries to God for forgiveness and help. It is a record of who we are.

God's merciful grace defies the standards we place upon ourselves and disrupts our assumptions on who should, or should not, be used by God. It is this honesty of life that Wesley spoke about so many times, one in which steps of human frailty led towards the divine. Simply put, it is a human record of His Love, and one that provides evidence for us all to continually walk its path of humility and grace.

The Groves ripple effect

Show Holmes a drop of water and he would deduce the
existence of the Atlantic. Show it to me and I would look for a tap.
That was the difference between us.

(Anthony Horowitz: *The House of Silk: Dr.Watson
talking about Sherlock Holmes*)

Anthony Norris Groves stepped off the boat that had brought him home to England. He was only in his late fifties, but time had taken its toll on his body and spirit. The years of faithful missions had finally caught up with him, and sickness had made permanent residence within his frail body.

A heavy blanket of disappointment afflicted him as he reviewed some of the treasures he had so deeply valued in life. The sacrifices made by his family and friends seemed to have left him with the haunting question, 'Was it really worth it?'

His treasured ideals had been smashed on the sharp rocks of life. Unity and love of fellow believers were all driving forces in his early years, but on his return he saw his beloved Brethren movement better known for infighting and disagreements than their communion around the Lord's Table. However painful this was, he was even more crushed by the news that few had followed his example of pursuing mission work abroad.

Mission was the Groves family's collective, driving passion. They delighted in demonstrating that God was faithful in sacrificial decisions, but were scarred by loss and hurt. They hoped that others would follow their life's service of compassion into a mission movement motivated not by income, status or role. They desired to flood the world with men and women daring to communicate the Gospel message, regardless of the personal cost. But Grove's return home proved that no such force existed.

His last few years in England could easily lead the observer to conclude that he was a broken man, who in 1853 left this world questioning the contribution he and his family had made. But the story doesn't end at his deathbed. Instead, it speaks of how sometimes we only truly see the full impact of our contribution when we rush into the welcoming arms of our Father.

A.N. Groves was born in 1795, in Hampshire, England, the only son of a family of six. His mother displayed a gentle compassion for those around, while his father's business ventures failed many times due to ill-advised enterprises. Committed Anglicans, the Groves family combined devoted religious service with committed determination, which soon rubbed off onto this growing teenage boy.

With a good education behind him, Groves began his career as a dentist. Shortly after his marriage to Mary Thompson, his practice achieved great success, and they committed to tithe their income to the poor. This offering increased as they found creative ways of living on the bare essentials, thus freeing up a substantial stream of income for charitable work. Eventually their exploration of the worshipful service of God led to the publication of a small booklet entitled *Christian Devotedness*, with its key verse, *'Lay not up for yourselves treasures upon earth'.*

Groves' childhood desire to become a missionary was rekindled. His wife Mary wasn't fully convinced of this new direction, but they waited patiently on God's guidance for a number of years, before both embarking on a path of overseas missions work. Resolved to work for the Christian Missionary Society, they gave up their secure income to begin training for ordination in a Dublin college, as this was a prerequisite of missionary work. During this time, a number of strange but divine events happened.

Groves crossed paths with fellow students, John Darby and John Bellett who had an intense study ethic and love for the classics. They were part of a growing number who were exploring the practice of meeting around the Lord's Table in their homes. This radical and controversial practice had already caused rumblings in the established church, but Groves recognised the beauty of unity that was budding in the early days of the Brethren movement. He joined in many discussions, exploring the practical outworking of these heart-felt ideas.

Meanwhile, Groves was having a painful debate with his mission society about the regulation that missionaries must be ordained as ministers. Both he and his wife had considered this rule limiting, as well as contrary to what they had concluded from the New Testament. When their savings were stolen, they painfully concluded that their actions must be guided by the Holy Spirit and not by the missionary board, so decided that they must abandon the society and hopes of ordination. This was a big step, as it immediately excluded them from organised support networks and the likelihood of a mission salary, but they had a simple, powerful belief in the faithfulness of God.

Giving their remaining possessions to the poor, they set sail as pioneering missionaries in June 1829. Landing in Russia, they then travelled through harsh terrain to their final destination, Baghdad. Without specific plans, Groves stated,

> I never had a very strong expectation that what we were to do was manifestly very great, but that we shall answer a purpose in God's plan I have no doubt (Dann, 2004).

The following year, a devastating plague hit the area. Starving children would roam the streets searching for food and help, the villagers struggling to clear the dead bodies that grew in devastating numbers. The local river then flooded its banks, devastating local homes and infrastructure. The resulting death toll was severe, and amongst the grieving was Groves himself, as he witnessed the death of his beloved wife and newborn daughter.

If that loss was not enough, soon after the plague had ended, the Turkish army invaded. With local government crippled, Groves and his remaining family had to survive with little communication or outside support from congregations. When asked later to recount those years, one of Groves' children responded that after leaving England he could not remember ever having been a boy.

Groves and his family pressed on, committed to the call despite these struggles and the questioning that had taken hold of his heart. As India opened up to mission work through the East India Company, in 1833 he was able to achieve a long-held desire to become a missionary to Asia. Here he stayed until his sad return home in 1852, and the year of soul searching before his death in May 1853. Yet this story does not end here.

While in India, Groves had mentored a young man called John Arulappan. He invested heavily in passing on his passionate beliefs about mission work and the pursuit of the gifts of the Holy Spirit. During his lifetime he saw his young Indian disciple step out into ministry, setting up assemblies in villages across the country. Yet this was only a precursor for something greater in years to come.

Arulappan would later be part of an outpouring of the Spirit in 1860, connecting streams of revival flowing through India. It was the start of a movement that would continue to sweep across the country, and become the backdrop of intercessory prayer that helped usher in the 1904 Welsh outpouring.

Another character in the story moved to London in 1829 for six months' training and while ill, came across Groves' booklet, *Christian Devotedness*. Later this challenging piece of writing took root in his life as he pondered how this couple had given up their income to become missionaries. This encouraged him to examine his own lifestyle, and seek further direction from God. His name was George Muller, famed for his sacrificial work with orphans and educational efforts among the poor. Years later, Groves would spend his dying days in this precious man's home.

Years after his death, Groves would be called 'the father of faith missions', a role model for future missionaries pursing a call of Christian devotion. It sparked a new movement of mission work that crossed denominational boundaries. Its ethos of compassion is perfectly summed up in Groves' humble booklet,

> Can we, with any truth, be said to love that neighbour as ourselves, who we suffer to starve whilst we have enough and to spare? (Groves, 2008).

I like to think of this story as the Groves ripple effect – the lasting impact of love's devoted service.

Thoughts

> A few moments later he put his hand over mine, and his eyes entreated me to draw closer to him. He uttered these words almost in my ear. And I am quite sure I have recorded them accurately, for his voice, though halting, was strangely distinct. 'Does it matter? Grace is everywhere'. I think he died just then.
>
> (Georges Bernanos: *The Diary of a Country Priest*, closing paragraph)

'Was it really worth it?' are not welcome words at the end of a life. In Grove's final two years, the joy of seeing his friend George Muller develop the growing orphanage work must have mingled with sorrow as he saw so much division in his circle of friends. He must have felt a sense of holy pride that his disciple was travelling the mission field of India, while he wept at the lack of interest back home for foreign missionary work.

Those five little words are weighty ones as we reflect on the story of Groves. We must examine our life's true impact with candour and honesty, and we need not run away from displays of weakness. Instead, we are invited by Christ to our own Gethsemane, to see that heaven's dreams in us are outworked in ways beyond human sight and expectation.

At Gethsemane Jesus, God but also man, felt the bitter wind of death. Its cold gusts gathered force, as he struggled with human weakness. Doubt, fear and uncertainty all must have figured in the painful scene in the garden.

At the cross our Saviour died at the hands of those he was expected to liberate his people from, and his dead body in the tomb seemed to declare another failed prophet and false hope. But the victory was just past earthly sight and the ripple effect of divine majesty has yet to reach its conclusion.

Yes, there is great joy in the final outcome, but the story of the cross suggests that not all harvests come before the dying breath. We want to taste the fruits of our labours while we live in this world, to see the results of our efforts and the confirmation of our success. Yet Jesus' cry at Gethsemane challenges our short-sightedness and reliance on limited human senses. His prayer declaring, *'Not my will, but yours be done'* (Luke 22:42), answers those five questioning words, 'Was it really worth it?'.

This prayer speaks of a higher desire, a line of sight beyond our understanding. It requires trust in God's guiding hand, and contentment even when not everything makes sense in our days on earth. It invites us to redefine our sense of timing and to be at peace with heaven's tempo, whatever that may be. Most of all, it asks us to be like children, just marvelling at the effect of a pebble in a pool.

Note 'B'
Prayer

Introduction: The anvil of prayer

They are hidden treasures, wrought in the darkness of dawn
and the heat of the noon on the anvil of experience, and beaten
into wondrous form by the mighty stroke of the divine.

(Claude L. Chilton: *The Complete Works of E.M. Bounds on Prayer*)

'My life is being crafted by God's hand' is a statement I have made
many times. Casually, even flippantly I have described my journey as a
pilgrim of faith who truly desires to change according to his will. It's
easy to say we are being moulded by divine love. But this process may
be anything but gentle and easy.

Imagine an anvil in the centre of a blacksmith's workshop. Rather
than a magnificent piece of industrial design, it is just a simple block
upon which an object is struck. It takes up less space than such large
structures as the forge or bellows. Yet this tool demonstrates a
fundamental principle of physics: inertia, the resistance to change.
The anvil is integral to the operation of the blacksmith, so that the
unseen picture in his mind can be made visible.

The moment when a static piece of metal resists the object being
fashioned upon it creates a forceful image. The blacksmith uses the fire
of the forge and the strength of the hammer to produce the intended
results. Change slowly occurs through intense heat, the skill of the
hand and continual beating on a forging block.

This is not a pleasant image of our Creator's interaction with us, but it is one of the notes in the symphony of revival when we consider our human resistance to change. Those believers who intercede through the night, who are caught up in the embrace of prayer, cry with determined passion for the fire and hammer. They yearn to go deeper when those who cherish comfort avoid it. They lay on the anvil their resistance to change, allowing the master craftsman to shape their lives and their world.

Stories of cherished revivals describe how prayer meetings and individual intercessors blanket the months and years prior to a divine moment, like the morning dew of heaven's touch. They may seem to indicate the importance of their role in that narrative, a blueprint that reveals the hidden design of revival. But to condense such journeys of devotion into a shortcut for hope bypasses the fearful element called 'personal cost', without which we are indeed the poorer.

The American E.M. Bounds faced this demand for a formula, as a man who discovered a helpful route of prayer. Bounds was born in 1835, and after a failed bid to find wealth in the gold rush, he followed in his fathers footsteps into the legal profession. At the age of nineteen he became Missouri's youngest lawyer, and seemed destined for a great career. Then he found himself in the middle of the Great Awakening, a move of God closely associated with people such as Dwight Lyman Moody. Believing he was called to preach, he left his position and studied for the ministry, soaking up the sermons of John Wesley.

Bounds' preaching commission began in a small-town church that was torn apart by the tensions of the American Civil War. Although adamantly opposing slavery, he refused to sign an oath of allegiance that he considered a state tactic to raise money and further division in the community. His actions were interpreted to mean he was a Confederate sympathiser, and he was held in a Federal prison for a year and a half. Released under a prisoner exchange programme, he was given an opportunity to be sworn in as a Confederate army chaplain.

Captured again during General Hood's defeat at Nashville, he was released by taking an oath of loyalty to the Union. Deciding to remain in the south, he committed his life to its spiritual and practical rebuilding. His journey later took him to Missouri, where he became the associated editor of the Methodist journal *The St Louis Advocate*, and was promoted soon afterwards to the national weekly Methodist paper *The Christian Advocate*.

Bounds' stories and editorial approach captured the passion for intercession that was running through the Methodist movement, and he became known to the public as a man who grasped the elusive element of prayer. Very soon the examples of the meetings he conducted with the Confederate army, and his commitment to early-morning intercession helped spark a spiritual awakening in the town where he worked as a pastor. They became beacons of hope for Christians to follow, a living example of the link between intercession and revival raining down on the land.

Bounds outlined his journey of prayer by dismantling some of the famous stories. He gave insights into the hidden trail of love, pointing each reader to the cost of devotion, requiring our all. He challenged formulas and exposed the simplicity of his routine of prayer in all its frail structure, focusing on what truly mattered, prayer being rooted in the heart.

Describing the pain of losing two of his children at the ages of one and six, he told of how prayer had entwined itself into the wholeness of life. Recounting nuggets of heavenly truth he mined during the times of pain and loss, he showed how questions and uncertainties were to be embraced as much as answers and surety.

These words were not an easy read for those who looked to his success in prayer. When he laid out in vivid detail what it was like to express sacrificial love in an environment alien to his own beliefs about slavery, he brought another level of reality to the journey of a pious life.

Despite numerous writings, by the time of his death in 1913, Bounds had only two books published on this subject. But with the help of his friends Homer W. Hodge and Claude L. Chilton, another nine manuscripts of his thoughts were later printed, providing nourishment for those hungry for spiritual truth.

In a foreword to one of those collections, Chilton speaks of his friend as a man:

> who prayed for long hours upon subjects to which the easy-going Christian rarely gives a thought . . . his solitary prayer vigils . . . took the command 'pray without ceasing' almost as literally as animate nature takes the law of the reflex nervous system which controls our breathing . . . as breathing is a physical reality to us, so prayer was a reality for Bounds (Bounds, 1990).

It was a fitting description of a man who continually challenged the perceptions of prayer, guiding those who heard his words towards a life-long journey of tears and joys.

The life of E.M. Bounds is a present-day challenge about the relationship between prayer and our revival hopes. It shows prayer as being rooted in the heart, a mirror reflecting the true nature of what lies within. Away from public gaze and bold statements of faith, is an act of worship that breaks the life we so cherish. Placing our being into the hands of our Maker, an inner cry yearns to be more like him. To truly be his hands and feet is a prayer of utter brokenness, as our compassion echoes the heartbeat of the one who made the ultimate sacrifice.

This picture of prayer recalls the image of the anvil, compact in the expanse of a blacksmith's workshop. We yearn for hopes of revival to come into being and our dreams to finally be fulfilled. But to enjoy the finished product, we must willingly lay our lives on the forging tool of prayer, allowing God to perform his work.

Those we hold up as heroes of prayer demonstrated a level of devotion beyond public words and vested interests. Their lives of utter commitment to Christ cost them everything, and the process of change broke their whole being. This cannot be taught, only lived, and each believer must decide how far they are willing to go.

The hidden prayer trail

By a series of steps of such remarkable guidance and wonderful coincidence that, so far as anything can be said to be wrought of God, with the least touch of human hand, so far it be said that God Himself arranged and brought to fruition the Convention which became one of the channels for the rivers of life to Wales.

(Jessie Penn-Lewis: *The Awakening in Wales*)

Dean Howell's breathing was becoming laboured, as the aged man took slow steps along the western coastline of his beloved Wales. His 83 years of life had taken a toll on his vigour, and the once thick skin that had handled cold winds now felt the bitter pinch between the gaps of his clothes. Although his movements were more considered, it didn't stop him taking this most treasured of walks, as he let the beauty of the horizon stir a passion in him.

He never got bored of this truly glorious sight. The waves crashing on the rocks, the jagged cliff edges resisting the constant process of erosion and weathering, and the vibrant sky declared in rich colours that only a divine hand could have painted such a canvas. It was a pastime he cherished, with each walk revealing something new of God's creative hand. But today was different, for in the depths of his spirit he knew this moment was commissioned to be something beyond the confines of his own mind.

Although his eyesight was fading, he took in the panoramic view, aware that soon he would step onto the shoreline of eternity. But he also knew his time was not up yet, and there was one message still to deliver. His frail eyes were about to gaze on a prophetic landscape that revealed the minuscule detail of his Father's work.

Rushing through the valleys like a low flying aircraft, his spirit's eye took in a snapshot of the events, gatherings, activities and prayers hidden from public sight. Something was afoot, dancing to a rhythm that only the spirit within seemed to catch; with participation from lovers of Christ but beyond anything humanly constructed. It expressed the Spirit's work, orchestrated through the conducting hand of the one true God.

As quickly as it started, Howell's focus returned to the shoreline where he first stood, the wind wrapping round his body and the cold air reddening his cheeks. He now understood the burden that lay in his soul. Returning home he penned an open letter to be published in a magazine in December 1902.

In it he called for a circle of intercessors who would entreat God to *'rend the heavens and come down'*. This was not a casual comment or fanciful idea, but a call to those who had not yet joined in with what he had already seen taking place across the valleys – the scattered huddles of prayer hidden away from public sight.

Howell's letter would later be defined as a prophetic statement for the Welsh revival of 1904. He closed it by stating:

> Take notice as if it were known that this was my last message to my fellow countrymen throughout the length and breadth of Wales before being summoned to judgment, and with the light of eternity already breaking over me. And it is this: the chief need of my country, of my dear nation at present, is a spiritual revival through a special outpouring of the Holy Ghost (Penn-Lewis, 1905).

A month after its publication, he stepped onto heaven's shoreline, but not before he was approached about a Keswick convention that was to take place in Llandrindod. This 'Conference for Wales' was still at an early stage and its proponents were unsure whether they could accomplish such a call for revival. So with trepidation the organisers came to the old man to garner his advice.

His response was to stand up and with hands raised towards heaven, said,

> I am an old man on the edge of eternity, and I say that if such a Conference could take place, God-given and not man-made, it would be an incalculable blessing to Wales (ibid, 1905).

The conference took place in 1903, and is ranked as a key event that helped usher Wales into revival's embrace. But its significance can only be truly appreciated when seen against the timeline of prayer guided by a divine hand.

In 1898 America, nearly four hundred people gathered together every Saturday night at the Moody Bible Institute to pray for a worldwide revival. Founded in 1886 by the evangelist D.L. Moody, this centre for missionary training had a vision to see God move within the Chicago locality and beyond. Committed faculty and students cried out to God, some continuing long past the allotted hours of the meeting.

As well as these gatherings, another band of people were praying for revival every Saturday night, this time in Australia. By a providential coincidence, a member of the Moody prayer group moved to Melbourne, unaware of what was taking place in the city. By 1901 the Australian prayer group had grown to over 40,000 people in 2,000 home prayer meetings, in 50 towns across the country.

The story of this amazing burden for revival was told in the Keswick convention held in the North East of England, 1902. It was an exceptional gathering for three reasons, the first being the burden of revival prayer that descended on the place. The second was that unbeknown to the attendees, an organic movement of a similar nature was already taking place in the United Kingdom, particularly in Wales. The third was that with an apparently supernatural recollection, people began to recount stories from the past that they had either heard or experienced, which when pieced together revealed a tapestry of divine work.

This fabric of connection was reflected in Howell's 'circle of implorers who would cry out the words of Isaiah' which he declared a few months later. In the collection of stories highlighted by the conference was the awareness of prayer groups which had emerged in India. With the same characteristics as the American, Australian and British groups, these home prayer meetings echoed a burden for intercession that seemed to have divine origins.

Two Welsh ministers, J. Rhys Davies and D. Wynne Evans, told how 13 Welsh people had met one day at the 1896 Keswick conference and prayed that God would give Wales its own 'Convention for Wales'. They continued to petition the Lord for a deepening of spiritual awareness in themselves and the nation, from that year onwards to that day in 1902.

In 1903, a few months after this story was shared, three Welsh ministers were stirred to pray together for God to move. They all carried a burden for national revival, but knew that the work must first start in their own hearts. So they faithfully gathered, though each one struggled to satisfy the stirring in their souls.

Seeking help, they wrote to a preacher whom they had heard speak about revival burdens. He pointed them towards a new conference that was to take place in August that year – the Convention for Wales. If they could attend, he would make time in his diary to pray with them and answer any questions that they had – and so it happened.

One of those three ministers was W.W. Lewis, who influenced a young preacher called Joseph Jenkins. Jenkins would later be known most famously for his meetings in Wales that explored how to 'deepen our loyalty to Christ'. In one of his meetings in 1904, a girl called Florrie Evans simply but powerfully declared, 'I love the Lord Jesus with all my heart'. This simple testimony later spread across Wales, affecting thousands of souls.

Another person who attended the Convention was a fiery preacher called Seth Joshua. At one meeting the weight of the Lord was so upon him for the nation of Wales, that he couldn't contain his petition any longer. His cry for Christ to 'bend me' had such an impact on a young man called Evan Roberts that it became the famous revivalist's own prayer and motto. 'O Lord, bend me' was a declaration that came to fruition on an October day in 1904.

We have little detail about what Howells saw prophetically that day in 1902. His published letter only gives hints about the circle of intercessors he had seen, an eclectic expression of prayer organised without human agency, a call for God to rend the heavens. In the space of two years the famous event at Moriah Chapel would take place, but this old man's sight was on another date entirely. He witnessed something that many of us don't get the privilege to see, God moving in the hidden realms.

Thoughts

> 'Cause when you move in me it's like a symphony, the timeless melody that soothes my soul. Though silent I can tell that you're alive and well, 'cause I can feel you move in me.
>
> (Michael W. Smith / Wayne Kirkpatrick: *Move in Me*)

These pages can never fully catch the complexity of the 1904 Welsh Revival. Whether through first-hand accounts, detailed historical critiques or inspirational writings, there is still a mystery about how this famous revival started.

Well-known figures like Evan Roberts, Seth Joshua, R.B. Jones and Joseph Jenkins joined in with other bands of preachers who invested in the nation of Wales before, during and after 1904. Then there were factors outside of the country itself, particularly the crusades of Dr. Reuben Torrey and Charles Alexander. Their meetings in Melbourne in 1902 built on an already strong burden of prayer, and ignited pockets of prayer all across the landscape. Although they were unable to spark a similar movement in Wales in 1904, the impact of the days of prayer and fasting was significant that year.

Every strand leads the inquisitive mind into a never-ending web of interwoven events and characters, each one contributing to something beyond the present. In the intersection of paths, a trail of prayer is detected that continues to be a central theme in many tales. From corporate gatherings to individual petitions, the road to the Welsh Revival was paved with pilgrims devoted to prayer.

Yet what stands out more than anything else is the divine nature of this call to action. Yes, there were times when the human ideas sparked initiatives, but most were prompted by the Spirit within. Without co-ordination other than from heaven's throne room, the build-up to that remarkable date was a symphony of prayer that seems impossible to fully grasp.

No one traveller knew entirely where this secret led, nor did any explorer have exclusive rights on that mysterious path. It is unsettling to the storyteller because whenever the starting point is found, the divine author points to another, earlier strand.

This is the beauty of the prayer trail. It dismantles the self-importance of thinking that our own prayer is the one that will usher in a move of God, while placing a priceless value on the integral part of our petition in the call for heaven's touch.

A crinkled newspaper clipping

The world has yet to see what God will do with a
man fully consecrated to Him.

(Henry 'Butcher' Varley)

It was only meant to be a few months of rest and recuperation in the United Kingdom, an opportunity to study Christian movements in a country other than his own. Dwight Lyman Moody, now in his thirties, had known both joy and disappointment in his growing ministry. His feet had walked a path of great promise, yet he had also stumbled along the way. After a testing time home in America, he was now venturing across the seas to find solace on new shores.

Moody had seen his father die in his childhood and experienced the seemingly endless struggle of a large family to survive on minimal income. While other children enjoyed playtime, he and some of his brothers and sisters had to work to support the family. As the years passed, working himself through a number of different jobs, he crossed paths with the famous missionary and writer Dr. Edward Norris Kirk, and a caring Sunday school teacher by the name of Edward Kimbell.

Dr. Kirk was a preacher deeply respected by Charles Finney as a fellow worker for revival. He placed his listeners in the melting pot of submission, using creative illustrations to amplify his message. As his ministry developed, demands increased, but he never failed to do his utmost for the lost, neglecting his own needs for the greater call of the Gospel message.

The young Moody attended church as a family duty, not because of a burning desire, and he had mixed feelings about Kirk's sermons. He occasionally fell asleep, upsetting older members of the congregation, but soon learned from their stern looks to pay attention to the respected pulpit. From then on, Kirk's words started to make an impact on his heart, but it was a simple act of love from Kimbell that shaped his life more than anything else.

Sitting in a Sunday school class, he was given a Bible and told to turn to the Gospel of John. He couldn't find it, and other children mocked as he flicked through the pages trying to find the elusive reference. The teacher called for silence and then offered his own open Bible in exchange for Moody's. Kimbell later recounted,

> I did not suppose the boy could possibly have noticed
> the glances exchanged between the other boys over his

ignorance, but it seems from remarks in later years that he did, and he said in reference to my little act in exchanging books that he would stick by the fellow who had stood by him and had done him a turn like that (Pollock, 1963).

Kimbell cared for all his young students, and not just on Sundays. He would regularly visit their homes and places of work throughout the week, taking interest in their activities and questions about life's struggles. He cared about their dreams and ideals, and was committed to see them live fully for Christ. And one day this led him to Moody's workplace, as Kimbell explains:

> When I was nearly there, I began to wonder whether I ought to go just then, during business hours. And I thought maybe my mission might embarrass the boy, that when I went away the other clerks might ask who I was, and when they learned might taunt Moody and ask if I was trying to make a good boy out of him. While I was pondering over it all, I passed the store without noticing it. Then when I found I had gone by the door, I determined to make a dash for it and have it over at once.

> I found Moody in the back part of the store wrapping up shoes in paper and putting them on shelves. I went up to him and put my hand on his shoulder, and as I leaned over I placed my foot upon a shoebox. Then I made my plea, and I feel that it was really a very weak one. I don't know just what words I used, nor could Mr. Moody tell. I simply told him of Christ's love for him and the love Christ wanted in return. That was all there was of it. I think Mr. Moody said afterwards that there were tears in my eyes (ibid, 1963).

Moody was seventeen when Kimbell led him to Christ. Remarkably, Moody in later years would lead a seventeen year old boy to Christ — the son of Edward Kimbell, his old Sunday school teacher.

Moody continued to succeed in the workplace, but he never forgot his childhood years of struggle and the impact of simple acts of care. He used his money to help children in need, whether renting pews so under-privileged boys had a place to worship, or hiring a carriage so a dying Sunday school teacher could carry out a desire to visit all the girls in her care: Moody was moved with compassion to communicate the Gospel.

He began to use his business connections to finance Gospel initiatives, until the Great Fire of 1871 destroyed much of his property. After great effort and personal attention, heartache and frustration, Moody and his team eventually saw their mission work rebuilt by 1872, but it had taken a toll on him.

Needing a break but also wanting to discover fresh ways of reaching the lost, he travelled to England that same year to combine some needed rest with learning. Persuaded by a London minister to preach in the city, Moody reluctantly accepted the offer, but the heavy smog dampened his enthusiasm. Yet his regret was soon replaced with joy, as nearly the entire congregation at the evening meeting at the Arundel Square Congregational Church near Pentonville Prison accepted Christ as their Saviour.

In the following few years, a series of trips to the United Kingdom propelled Moody's ministry to a whole new level, as his partnership with the singer Ira D. Sankey creatively blended the arts with evangelism. The popularity of the gatherings meant that in some cases special trains were laid on for those attending. At the Botanic Garden Palace in Glasgow, Moody preached from a carriage and the choir had to sing from a shed rooftop because of the vast crowds. At Arthur's Seat in Edinburgh, an estimated 20,000 came to hear the gospel.

These were just two of the meetings that became talking points in the country and beyond, and proved to be a training ground for Moody and Sankey. But woven into the accounts of salvation calls is the story of a bedridden lady.

Turning the clock back to Moody's London holiday of 1872, a lady called Marianne Adlard was visited by her older sister, excitedly relaying the news that 'Moody of America' had just preached at her Congregationalist church in Arundel Square. The invalid woman responded that she knew what that meant. God had heard her prayers. She pulled from under her pillow a faded and crinkled newspaper clipping of Moody's activities in Chicago and handed it to her sister. For years she had been praying for him to visit her church, and now that prayer had blossomed.

Thoughts

> The unfinished picture would so like to jump off
> the easel and have a look at itself.
>
> (C.S. Lewis: *Letters to Malcolm*)

In his *Letters to Malcolm*, C.S. Lewis battled with the tension between faith and logic: the interweaving paths that the praying believer must continually choose between. A blinkered approach to faith could lack authenticity, but staying in the rigid confines of logic would limit the Christian walk. Somewhere in between is respect for both; a deep prayerfulness but a clear understanding of the world, without conforming to the world's 'norm'.

Marianne Adlard's crinkled newspaper clipping was more than a visual representation of an answered prayer. The creased, torn sheet spoke of a precious aspect of our faith – commitment. This gemstone of untold value is formed over time, away from public gaze, as the praying believer persistently makes their petition. And commitment is truly tested when it walks on the path of both faith and logic.

Logic on its own might highlight the improbability of an American preacher finding his way to another country to visit a church he has no idea exists. It would question how the humble prayer of a bedridden individual could influence such a task, rather than, perhaps, a letter writing campaign to grab the attention of Moody and his team.

Yet logic spurred the prayer for a notable preacher to grace the footsteps of her home church. Against all earthly probability Adlard believed that Moody would come, but her commitment to pray was tested over the course of years with no response. The newspaper clipping was visible evidence, yet beyond earthly sight was the hand of the Almighty influencing events.

Moody's inner questions about mission work which led him to the UK were unrelated to Adlard's prayer, yet were used in God's providence to answer it. A further dimension of this divine connection is revealed in a famous quotation, first voiced by Henry 'Butcher' Varley during the years of Adlard's intercession. After a night-long prayer meeting, Butcher told Moody that the world needed to see a man fully consecrated to the purposes of God.

Moody made no comment at the time, but digested those words deep inside. By the time he arrived in London and sat in the gallery of Spurgeon's Metropolitan Tabernacle, his mind was set to pursue that challenge. It would only be a matter of days before he saw what a man fully consecrated to God could achieve.

The old but sure message

I love to tell the story of unseen things above,
of Jesus and His Glory, of Jesus and His Love.

I love to tell the story, because I know 'tis true,
it satisfies my longings as nothing else can do.

(Katherine Hankey: *I Love to Tell the Story*)

William P. Lockhart held his pen with prayerful consideration, remembering words shaped through the years. In letters, papers and sermons, messages of joy and pain, celebration and concern had all been created on the desk he now sat behind. It was an oasis for him, this writing sanctuary, where he could reflect on all that was within. While some enjoyed walks or moments of silent retreat to hear the quiet words of Christ, for Lockhart the dance of the pen on the page quieted his mind as nothing else did.

Yet today was different as the letter he was writing had a heaviness to it. After only a few words, his hand stopped because of the turmoil within his heart. He knew this was going to be difficult task; a challenge he wished could pass. Yet this message to his friend that would be an open letter to the church in general, needed to be written.

The thoughts he would convey had been etched into his heart through personal experience. He was in his late fifties now, but ever since young adulthood, Lockhart had devoted himself to God and the work of salvation. Born in 1835, he moved from Scotland with his family at the age of eleven, eventually settling in Birkenhead, Liverpool. Although he knew the Bible throughout his childhood years, it wasn't until the age of twenty that he gave his heart to the Lord.

A visit to Wales in 1855 had prompted a memory of his apprenticeship in Paris during his late teens. That trip to France was intended for perfecting his language and business skills, but one event dominated it more than anything else. He was staying with the family of a clergyman who frequently challenged Lockhart about his faith. This became acutely real as an outbreak of typhus took hold of the city where his lodgings were. It wasn't long before the dark cloak of the disease caused death to some in the household.

While the twenty-year old Lockhart walked through the picturesque Welsh landscape, his mind was caught up in vivid memories of that vulnerable time. As the challenging words from the clergyman's family began once again to ring in his ears, the image of Jesus on the cross suddenly appeared before his eyes. In graphic reality that could not be ignored, the words *'It is finished'* brought him to his knees. By the narrow stretch of waters called the Menai Strait he knew what he must do, and turning his face towards heaven he gave his life into the hands of Christ.

Lockhart was unaware that this moment was part of a wider story being played out in the land of Wales and beyond. For the next four years there were uncanny incidents of people recalling interactions with people who had shared the Gospel message with them in years gone by. By the time a preacher delivered his sermon, many had already made a decision in their heart, only responding to the altar call to confirm what had already taken place.

This divine interaction between the created and the Creator was only realised because of the thorough follow-up carried out by local churches. Before someone could truly call themselves 'saved', they were examined over four to eight weeks. A church member would interview the 'repented' individual's family, work colleagues, neighbours and friends, to gauge what type of journey they had been on.

Once satisfied that a person's life had truly changed, the church would then intensively question them about their journey to faith. By the time this process had finished, many congregations had started to recognise an emerging trend.

Initially they assumed that salvation came through the sermon and the altar call, but it became evident that the new believers had in common a supernatural experience of remembrance. They might then come to a meeting and respond to the preacher's call, thinking that this was how it needed be done. Incidences of this testimony increased over the coming years, eventually becoming a bedrock of the Welsh and Scottish Revivals of 1858.

This supernatural touch led Lockhart to sit under the ministry of Hugh Stowell Brown, a passionate and provocative preacher who was committed to social reform. With initiatives such as the development of localised banks to help with money management and education, Lockhart strengthened his resolve to 'not sleep in the church, but throw his whole soul into the cause'.

This was an exciting time as this work grew from strength to strength, often testifying to how practical needs were addressed through social action projects. Yet as time went on, questions began to emerge during his times of prayer about his work at the coalface of poverty. While he had met practical needs, he had not quenched spiritual need in the community. Many had drunk water from his cup, but few had really tasted from the stream of life itself.

With each passionate plea Brown gave for his congregation to press into social action, Lockhart continued to address his inner turmoil:

> I derive very much benefit and instruction from Mr. Brown's preaching and ought to be very thankful that I am privileged to sit under such a minister. The only improvement I could wish to see is a little more preaching mixed up with the teaching (Green, 2010).

The more time he spent in prayer, the greater he felt, 'how great the blame attachable to those who neglect to continually direct their hearers to the Lamb of God who taketh away the sins of the world'.

Being a keen sportsman he found many opportunities to share the gospel. His cricketing skills opened up many doors for people to listen to his words, but time and time again he felt overwhelmed. He still struggled with his conclusion that the call every believer has to share the Gospel message must never be treated casually. This sober responsibility to do with eternity and the cross grew heavy in him.

Determined to overcome such concerns, he devised a notebook to help him more effectively share the love of Christ. Inside it he recorded the date, name and topic of conversations he had with people, as well as what he needed to bring in prayer. It was designed to not let him off the hook, and it worked. It became very rare to have a blank page on any day.

In 1859 a chance conversation on a ferry led to the suggestion that a branch of a new initiative, the Young Men's Christian Association (YMCA) should be opened up in Birkenhead. During some exploratory meetings, Lockhart met a man called Charles Webb who held a weekly prayer and study group. This work focused on seeking an outpouring of God in their locality.

Webb knew straightaway that Lockhart's passionate insight into prayer and evangelism would be a great addition to their quest. Inviting him to preach early in 1860, Lockhart's 35-minute sermon on the subject of 'What must I do to be saved?' had a powerful impact on his listeners. Asked again to preach two weeks later, he initially refused, stating that he had nothing left to say. Webb eventually convinced Lockhart to come back and preach the same sermon again – and the results were replicated.

Soon Lockhart was preaching each week for this group seeking revival in their town. Before his eyes he saw people getting themselves right before God and hardened characters weeping for salvation, as business and social conditions greatly improved. As Lockhart travelled back and forth from Scotland whilst keeping up to date with news coming out of Wales, he noted how his local town folk were anxious for the state of their souls, joining in a heavenly movement happening across the land. Over the space of five years, at least one million souls were saved.

Challenged by Spurgeon's question, 'Can none of you young men do something for religion in the places you live?' Lockhart began a series of local evangelistic meetings in his home city of Liverpool. The work grew and was eventually housed in the Hengler's Circus building, a chain of properties built and run by Charles Hengler. Unlike the circus entertainment of the former inhabitants, they used no instruments at all, instead relying upon volunteer participation and Spirit-led singing.

Lockhart then preached on his 'Circus Subjects', a series of sermons about inner conviction and outward mission. At one of those meetings he was introduced to an unknown American preacher on an exploratory trip around the country, who was then invited to say a few words in the Circus. History records this as the first sermon preached on English soil by an up-and-coming evangelist, D.L. Moody.

During this outpouring of God's grace, he noted how the qualitative work of God went past man's desire for just the quantity of responses and hands raised. This thought remained with him throughout his life, and one that struck the loudest chord as he sat in front of his writing desk. It reminded him deep in his soul that transformation comes from the conviction of the Holy Spirit, which must never be avoided or substituted for easier means.

Over the years he had noticed a new term appearing in Christian dialogue – the 'Social Gospel', describing a growing movement of social engagement. This was a collection of different voices with diverse theologies, all expressing how the prayer *'Your kingdom come'* could be relevant in society. It would have a lasting effect on someone taking the stage at the Lincoln Memorial in Washington some sixty years later. Influenced by the early teachings of this movement, Martin Luther King, Jr. eventually translated its words into the world-famous speech, 'I have a dream'.

Lockhart had always believed in social action, and worked in some of the poorest areas of the city for his last thirty years of ministry. But he was very concerned about the amount of attention this aspect of Christian living was being given. He feared that the directness of the Gospel message was being replaced by more seeker-friendly sermons on ecology, economics and radical political ideas.

Lockhart's prayerful heart convinced him that the starting block was not a change of circumstance, but a change of heart, and if the church lost sight of that then it would be nothing more than another protesting body. It was a controversial viewpoint, particularly in a time when there was a rising interest in the power of the church to address social issues. His stance was often misunderstood, but he never shied away from speaking his mind in a heartfelt way.

This was one of those moments, as he lovingly crafted the letter to his friend in 1892.

> The old Gospel as you call it, is rather at a discount just now, and many are the difficulties on every hand. We are surrounded with them here. What with social gospel, and rubbish about land and wages, and pleasant Sunday afternoons, with solo-singers applauded and encore-d, bands, and historical lectures – all these at Sunday services – the young people are being enticed away from everything solid and helpful.

> Then also there is an undercurrent of doubt about everything that is dangerously insidious. Still, there have been always these things, or their first cousins, more or less. We must cast ourselves more and more upon God, and seek His strength. The most painful feature is that these things are affecting the life of God's own children. We must not, however, despair.

> I keep on at the old thing. Delivered fifteen Sunday morning lectures lately on the Epistle of Jude, and our people licked their lips over them, showing that love for the truth has not disappeared. It is a testing time, as if God were watching to see whom among His children will stand fast.

> The Lord keep us. There will be a revival of old Puritan doctrine before long, of which I am sure, though you and I many not live to see it. God is alive, and will yet stretch out His Hand and vindicate His own truth (ibid, 2010).

Two weeks after he wrote the letter, he was bedridden due to a ruptured blood vessel and on the 12th August 1893 at the age of fifty-seven, Lockhart fell into the embrace of his welcoming Father. *The Liverpool Daily Post* paid its respect through the most beautiful of homages:

> In these days, when it is often and foolishly said that men do nothing entirely without reference to gain, there is consolation in regarding such a life as closed on Saturday, when W.P. Lockhart as he was always called gave his pure soul unto his Captain Christi, under whose colours he had fought so long. The great volunteer preacher passed away after the briefest of retirement, expected to be only temporary, from public and private labour . . .

> He had great preaching gifts, a lucid style, a penetrating and sensitive voice, a natural aptitude for popular reform and incapability of being dull, considerable effectiveness in illustration, and a happy though restrained fecundity in anecdote. He really was a great citizen, pure, earnest, philanthropic, full of faith that only Christianity could cure the ills of the world . . . (Liverpool Daily Post archives).

Thoughts

> One act of a good man's life may differ widely from another in importance. Paul's sewing of tents was not equal to his writing an Epistle to the Romans, but both were accepted of God and both were true acts of worship. Certainly it is more important to lead a soul to Christ than to plant a garden, but the planting of the garden can be as holy an act as the winning of a soul.
>
> (A.W. Tozer: *The Pursuit of God*)

There is a day that I will always remember, over a decade ago. I had the privilege of spending time with an elderly man who had breathed in the fragrance of the Isle of Lewis revival in 1949. When asked why he thought the revival started and what caused it to seemingly dwindle away in the early 50's, he responded, 'It's a mystery . . . but what I do know is this . . .' (Smithyman, 2013).

He then went on to describe the years before that famous time, when the church sought to serve the community through various programmes and activities. Despite some success, many came to realise that their carefully planned activities could not fully meet the needs of the pain they saw firsthand.

Exposure to the dark corners of their neighbourhoods brought a different dimension to their prayers. No more were they just words from the comfort of their tidy surroundings, now it was raised hands that carried the grime of the streets and the scars of mission work. There was a desperation in their collective intercession and the knowledge that only God could answer their cries. What persisted for hours, days, months, and then years, was finally answered in November 1949.

The common factor of the revival was passionate prayer in utter dependence on Christ, while never evading responsibility for their neighbours. Recalling those rare and precious times brought tears to his eyes, but soon also disappointment and a sense of loss. He ended his thoughts with a statement that has never left my mind, and one that seems to explain the sadness I witnessed that day.

> You know young man, before the revival happened, more people attended those prayer times than the meetings themselves. By the time the revival finished, more people attended the praise meetings than those times of petition (ibid, 2013).

Prayer and social action: it seems to be one of those fragile partnerships in which each party clamours for prominence. They both have their supporters who acknowledge the other's contribution, yet compete for importance. This fragile union seems to reflect the intricate nature of our faith, which is an organic relationship of the bended knee and blistered hand. When they are moulded into unity, a divine work of art is displayed.

The landscape of history flowers with vivid colours of sacrificial works and kind acts. It is tempting to stare on such magnificence, and praise its splendour as though it is the height of creation's work. Yet I learned a lesson that day from the elderly man, that the garden of prayer provides the ground for such beauty to blossom. It is a partnership of private creation and public display, intimately entwined.

Conclusion: the dissonance note

Earth's crammed with heaven, and every common bush
afire with God; But only he who sees, takes off his shoes –
The rest sit round it and pluck blackberries.

(Elizabeth Barrett Browning: *Aurora Leigh*)

A pilgrim gazes on the course ahead, his eyes darting between the vast landscape before him and the map in his hands. The path he stands upon seems straight and level, the surface welcoming to his feet; but looking into the distance reveals the incline of the land and a meandering route that becomes uneven and intricate as it unfolds. Glancing down, his map outlines the planned journey, highlighting the various altars of remembrance positioned along *the way*.

To a traveller like this pilgrim who has only heard tales of this precious journey yet until now never embarked on completing its course, these marked-out sacred spaces are priceless. They are stepping-stones along *the way* that guide the pilgrim towards his final destination.

These signposts are variably constructed, from elaborate monuments of corporate worship to humbly crafted prayers. Yet regardless of their outward appearance, each one signals a period of precious reflection which then propels the pilgrim forward to the next stage of his devotional journey.

The pilgrim's map has been prepared with great care, combining directions for the journey, and encouragement to soak in the atmosphere of discovery along the way. At first glance the chart could give the impression that the expedition is as simple as 'a' to 'b' to 'c', and that the meaning of each altar is defined by its title. But the pilgrimage is a mystery that no map can fully define, and any guide constructed by human hands is just that, 'a guide', helping but not dictating.

To fully understand the meaning of the journey, each person needs to experience the walk personally; to be guided by the route markings yet soak in the life found along the way. As the pilgrim takes his first step, he looks at the map once more before folding it up until it will be called upon again. This printed guide points towards his initial route, but only hints at what mysteries lay ahead – where the journey itself defines the goal he seeks.

* * * * *

This book records monuments of remembrance on the map of revival's symphony – storytelling, activism, obedience, daily life, the architecture of connections, precious weakness, and prayer. The map it creates is a musical scale, respecting our need to put things into a theological scale whilst praising the beauty that the life of music carries: unity in diversity. Yet my structure of seven themes also reveals a flaw, the exclusion of other treasured aspects of the revival narrative such as miraculous moments, hidden years of activity, and a greater emphasis upon the divine. I am glad my Heptatonic scale has imperfection, as it highlights to me in vivid reality the vastness of heaven's symphony and the limitation of the mind to comprehend it. C.S. Lewis articulated it so wonderfully within his Narnia books, when he likened our journey of faith to that of such things as a wardrobe or picture frame. Our assumption is that we know what these objects are for, but when approached through the vista of a child's mind, a whole new world is laid out before us: a landscape of wonder and beauty, a panorama of narration and sound that is missed through the eyes of presupposition.

Like the sermon outlined in the preface, for many years I imagined how revival should look. In my mind's eye a map was laid out, marking each action that a believer should perform to establish the right environment for a move of God. Once done, then God would provide that final divine moment which no human deed could provoke. It was a comfortable image that gave me assurance, a utopian hope that all would be fine as long as I did my pre-defined part.

These 'altars of action' for revival can differ for each one of us. For some they could signify prayer or the preaching of the word of God, for others pursuing holiness or a way of worship both corporate and individual. But what if our assumptions of what these alters mean distract us from the joy of the pilgrimage itself? Could we be missing the Designer's plan if our desire to reach each goal results in us running as fast as we can, ticking off each altar? Our goals can be precious, our definitions valuable, but let us never lose sight that revival's symphony is a living and evolving sound of worshipful interaction which challenges our desire for a clear-cut path.

This leads me to reflect on the theme of music once again. Caught within the dynamics of any musical scale is the uncomfortable space of dissonance: the lack of harmony, a note that seems out of place. This temporary relationship of played notes can seem awkward, disjointed from the assumed sequence of tones. It has a different DNA; as if it is a mistake. It stands out as an incorrect note or disrupting sound, even if it is a purposeful decision of the musician to dislodge the expected musical sequence.

Dissonance is hard to pin down, as it isn't confined to one specific note. Instead it exists within the musical piece itself, because if placed within another piece of music those notes would no longer be discordant. The elusive, ever-moving and fluid energy cannot be fixed on a page; it surprises us as it attaches onto a note and then dances off to another bar of evolving music.

It is intended as a creative element to expand the experience and imagination. Yet it can stand out and be an uncomfortable space to dwell in. It may not make sense, and may cause us to wriggle in our seats or grimace.

This is a less than romantic image of something that is integral to the overall completed sound that we are to enjoy. Contrary to its perception of discord it can produce a harmony, but this can only be recognised in the context of the overall musical piece. It puts a demand on the listener to trust the journey itself to bring forth its meaning along the way.

This paradox of disruption as an integral ingredient of the unified whole seems perfectly captured by a talk given by a filmmaker in 2007. In his speech, J.J. Abrams spoke of a childhood visit he made to the magic shop in New York City called Lou Tannen's Magic. There he bought the

> Tannen's Mystery Magic Box ... 'Fifteen dollars buys you fifty dollars worth of magic'. If you look at this, you'll see that it's never been opened. But I've had this forever. And I realised that I haven't opened it because it represents something important to me ... it represents infinite possibility. Now it's not the most groundbreaking idea, but maybe there are times where mystery is more important than knowledge.

Mystery invites us to take stock of the environment that it resides itself in, to see that the inconvenience of any elusive answer is part of the very life and discovery of what we truly seek. This is what I believe the dissonance tone of revival is: mystery of the divine. An enigma that we want to solve yet seems to be beyond the confines of our language and any constructed plan.

> *"Much that God is doing looks to us like an accident or a mistake. Due to our blindness and our ignorance, we do*

not know why God is doing what He is doing, and so we begin to fidget and wonder if God does really know. However, God sees tomorrow; we see only today. God sees both sides; we see only one side. God knows that we do not know and God has all the pieces to the puzzle; you and I have only a few ... Here is our pattern of life, and we like to see it bloom into a beautiful picture where everything is in place; but it has all (been) scattered around and we do not know where the pieces are; nothing fits ... People do not like the word 'mystery', but it is a good Bible word, and it is a word we ought to learn to live with. For the world - everything around about us - is shrouded in mystery. Regarding things concealed, Lady Julian wrote 'And I saw not the creature doing, but I saw God doing in the creature' ... " (Tozer, 2009)

So why is mystery so integral to revival? It reminds us that a move of God is more than a rigid journey from 'a' to 'c', questioning our definitions of hope being out-worked in pre-determined ways. It trips up our rushing steps and makes us slow down to notice the hints and whispers that shape the answers we seek. Mystery challenges our bias and expectations, shining a light upon our vested interests. It reminds us of the question, *"Can anything good come out of Nazareth?"* as it dislodges our preference to simplify the revival story to a date, location and heroic figure. The stage curtain is drawn back to reveal characters missed by the narrowness of our storytelling, and speaks of another language to interpret what we see. Mystery declares that this language is love, a puzzling discovery of compassion that displays its majesty in various ways.

Love strikes at our motives, removes any status and questions the line that separates the sacred and secular. Love is to be experienced, to be lived, and to lay down one's self for. It surrounds our pilgrimage path and is the air that we as travellers breathe in. It is the motivation of our actions and the energy in our deeds, the voice in our prayers and the backbone of our commitment. When revival is seen through the eyes of love, we truly do relish in the mystery of its expression. A world impacted by the active demonstration of divine passion, way beyond the confines of a wardrobe or picture frame.

So live well and dare to explore. Breathe in Love's fragrance and let its passion continually take us off our expected route. Brave the elements and never be afraid of the questions provoked. Pursue the

Spirit of God but avoid the temptation of formulas and emotional quick fixes. Embrace the journey of love and let that be the motivation of all deeds. Enjoy its interactive sound and share it tones to the world around, applauding its life but never limiting its impact upon hearts seeking a heavenly Saviour. Above all, be the musician in revival's symphony, this stunning masterpiece crafted by a divine Hand and Mind – a piece of music so exquisitely written that its notes captures the attention of The Composer's created world.

Author's Closing Thoughts

I'd rather be a comma than a full stop. Maybe I'm in the black,
maybe I'm on my knees. Maybe I'm in the gap between
the two trapezes, but my heart is beating and my
pulses start: Cathedrals in my heart.

(Coldplay: *Every Teardrop Is A Waterfall*)

I never set out in these pages to define revival. I acknowledge and honour that within the bookshelves of history and within our family homes are ample pieces of literature that have already explored this subject far more thoroughly than myself. Instead, my prayer is that this book encourages us all, including myself, to stop and take a breath.

The Kingdom work of Christ that we see only in part, acts as a comma in a sentence that is being crafted by God's loving Hand – a rest in His musical composition. In this pause of reflection, it tells us that revival is not a destination or an outcome that we work towards; neither is it a utopian hope that lets us off the hook with set aside prayer meetings and pulpit sermons. Rather, it is a journey that is travelled that continually reminds us of the greatest commandments of our faith. *"Love the Lord your God with all your passion and prayer and intelligence. This is the most important, the first on any list. But there is a second to set alongside it. Love others as well as you love yourself. These two commands are pegs; everything in God's Law and the Prophets hangs from them"* (Matthew 22:37-40 Message).

This *infinite demand of love* is the gap between the two trapezes of what we know and what we hope for. It takes us past any theoretical knowledge and challenges any excuse upon waiting for the future.

> What is being called for is a rigorous and activist conception
> of faith that proclaims itself into being at each instant
> without guarantee or security, and which abides with the
> infinite demand of love (Critchley, 2012).

This places us in the now, in the open air of uncertainty. And maybe just then, when all we can rely upon is the motivation of that demand, we will hear something beautiful – a symphony that has never ceased from being played, impacting the world through revival's precious tones of love.

Further information and downloadable content
(including study guide) available at:

www.mysongmedia.co.uk
www.andysmithyman.co.uk

BIBLIOGRAPHY:

Allen, A. (1957) *My Cross: the life story of A.A. Allen as told by himself*. Hereford Miracle Valley: A.A. Allen Revivals.

Archer, M. (2003) *Structure, agency and the internal conversation*. Cambridge: Cambridge University Press.

Badiou, A. (2012) *In praise of love. London*: Profile Books Ltd.

Bernanos, G. (1983) *The diary of a country priest*. New York: Carroll and Graf Publishers Inc.

Biehl, J. (1998) *The politics of social ecology: libertarian municipalism*. London: Black Rose Books.

Booth, W. (1890) *In darkest England and the way out*. Reprint: Stafford: Forgotten Books, 2011.

Booth, W. (1891) *Twenty-One years' Salvation Army*. Reprint, Boston: Adamant Media Corp, 2005.

Boulton, E.C.W. (1999) *George Jeffreys: a ministry of the miraculous*. Tonbridge: Sovereign World Ltd.

Bounds, E. M. (1990) *The complete works of E.M. Bounds on prayer*. 4th edn. Grand Rapids: Baker Books.

Bouge, D & Bennett, J. (1810) *History of dissenters: from the revolution in 1688 to the year 1808*. Newport: R. Tilling.

Buchanan, M. (2002) *Nexus: Small Worlds and the groundbreaking science of networks*. New York: W.W. Norton and Company, Inc.

Buck, C. (1822) *Works of the reverend Charles Buck: late minister of the Gospel*. Philadelphia: W.W. Woodward.

Bunyan, J. (1917) *The Holy war*. London: Ward, Lock & Company Ltd.

Bunyan, J. (1921) *The pilgrim's progress*. Reprint, Letchworth: Temple Press.

Burke, K. (1973) *The philosophy of literary form*. 3rd edn. California: The Regents.

Cadbury, D. (2010) *Chocolate wars: from Cadbury to Kraft, 200 years of sweet success and bitter rivalry*. London: Harperpress.

Campbell, J. (2008) *The hero with a thousand faces*. 3rd edn. Novato: New World Library.

Chomsky, N. (2007) *On language: language and responsibility, reflections on language*. New York: The New Press.

Chomsky, N. (2009) *Chomsky on anarchism*. Edinburgh: AK Press.

Coutts, F. (1974) *No discharge in this war: a one volume history of The Salvation Army*. London: Hodder and Stoughton Ltd.

Critchley, S. (2012) *The faith of the faithless: experiments in political theology*. New York: Verso.

Crystal, D. (ed.) (1998) *The Cambridge biographical encyclopedia*. 2nd edn. Cambridge: Cambridge University Press.

Dallimore, A.A. (1990) *George Whitefield: God's anointed servant in the great revival of the eighteenth revival*. Illinois: Crossway Books.

Dann, R.B. (2004) *Father of faith missions: the life and time of Anthony Norris Groves*. Milton Keynes: Authentic Media.

Davies, R. E. (1963) *Methodism*. Harmondsworth: Penguin Books.

Dickens, C. (1922) *A Christmas carol*. Reprint, London: Miller, Son and Company, 2011.

Doddridge, P. (2011) *The rise and progress of religion in the soul*. Michigan: Waymark Books.

Dorsett, L.W. (1997) *The life of D.L. Moody: a passion for souls*. Chicago: Moody publishers.

Drummond, L. (1992) *Spurgeon: prince of preachers*. Michigan: Kregel Publications.

Dunn, J.D.G. (2006) *Unity and diversity in the New Testament: an inquiry into the character of earliest Christianity*. 3rd edn. Norwich: SCM Press.

Edsor, A. (1989) *Set your house in order: God's call to George Jeffreys as the founder of the Elim Pentecostal movement*. Chichester: New Wine Press.

Edwards, J. (2007) *Life and diary of David Brainerd*. New York: Cosimo Inc.

Epstein, D.M. (1993) *Sister Aimee: the life of Aimee Semple McPherson*. London: Harcourt Brace and Company.

Evans, E. (1979) *Revival comes to Wales: the story of the 1859 revival in Wales*. 3rd edn. Bridgend: The Evangelical Press of Wales.

Evans, E. (1985) *Daniel Rowland and the great Evangelical awakening in Wales*. Edinburgh: The Banner of Truth Trust.

Evans, E. (1996) *Fire in the thatch*. Bridgend: The Evangelical Press Of Wales.

Evans, E. (1996) *Pursued by God: a selective translation with notes of the Welsh classic Theomemphus by William Williams of Pantycelyn*. Bridgend: The Evangelical Press of Wales.

Finney, C.G. (1979) *Reflections on revival*. Michigan: Bethany House Publishers.

Fisher, W.R. (1989) *Human communication as a narration: toward a philosophy of reason, value, and action*. Columbia: University of South Carolina Press.

Fraser, D. (1973) *The evolution of the British welfare state*. 3rd edn. Basingstoke: Palgrave MacMillan.

Gadamer, H. (1975) *Truth and method*. Reprint, London: Continuum International Publishing Group, 2004.

Gardiner, A.G. (1923) *Life of George Cadbury*. London: Cassell and Company.

Goldberg, M.C. (1998) *The art of the question: a guide to short-term question-centered therapy*. New York: John Wiley and Sons Ltd.

Green, G.R. (2010) *Liverpool gripped by revival*. Merseyside: Green.

Groves, A.N (1832) *Journal of a residence Bagdad, during the years 1830 - 1831*. Reprint: Stafford: Forgotten Books, 2012.

Groves, A.N (2008) *Christian devotedness: or the consideration of our Saviour's precept "Lay not up for yourselves treasures upon earth"*. Utah: Project Gutenberg.

Hallett, M & Riding, C. (2006) *Hogarth*. London: Tate Publishing.

Hardman, K.J. (1987) *Charles Grandison Finney: revivalist and reformer*. Reprint, Grand Rapids: Baker Book House Company, 1990.

Harris, B. (2004) *The origins of the British welfare state: social welfare in England and Wales, 1800 - 1945*. Basingstoke: Palgrave MacMillan.

Harrison, F. M. (1928) *John Bunyan: a story of his life*. Reprint, London: The Banner of Truth Trust, 1964.

Harvey, W. (1906) *The model village and its cottages: Bournville*. Reprint, Milton Keyness: Lightening Source UK Ltd, 2011.

Hattersely, R. (1999) *Blood and fire: William and Catherine Booth and the Salvation Army*. London: Abacus.

Hill, C. (1972) *The world turned upside down: radical ideas during the English revolution*. Reprint, London: Penguin Books, 1991.

Hitt, J. (2005) *Off the road: a modern-day walk down the pilgrim's route into Spain*. New York: Simon and Schuster Paperbacks.

Jackson, T. ed (1831) *The works of John Wesley*. Reprint, Massachusetts: Hendrickson Publishers, 1991.

Jones, D. (1902) *Life and times of Griffith Jones of Llanddowror*. Reprint, Hartshill, Tentmaker Publications, 1995.

Jones, R.B (1931) *Rent heavens: the revival of 1904*. Reprint, London: Pioneer Mission, 1948.

Massey, R. (1992) *Another Springtime: Donald Gee*. Surrey: Highland Books.

Milton, J. (2004) *Paradise lost. Oxford*: Oxford University Press.

Moody, D.L. (1891) *Sovereign grace*. Reprint, Chicago: The Moody Bible Institute, 1998.

Moody, D.L. (approx 1890) *The way to God: a series of addresses*. London: Morgan & Scott.

Murray, I.H. (1972) *Forgotten Spurgeon*. Edinburgh: The Banner of Truth Trust.

Murray, I.H. (1987) *Jonathan Edwards: a new biography*. Reprint, Edinburgh, The Banner of Truth Trust, 2000.

Nevinson, H.W. (1895) *Neighbors of ours: slum stories of London*. Reprint, Stafford: Forgotten Books, 2012.

Nevinson, H.W. *The new slave trade: Harpers Monthly Magazine*. August 1905 to February 1906.

Nickalls, J. L. (ed.) (1952) *The journal of George Fox*. Reprint, Philadelphia: Philadelphia Yearly Meeting of the Religious Society of Friends, 1997.

Penn-Lewis, J. (1905) *The awakening in Wales*. Reprint, Fort Washington: CLC Publications, 2002.

Phillips, T. (1860) *The Welsh revival: its origin and development*. Reprint, Edinburgh: The Banner of Truth Trust, 1995.

Pierson, A.T. (1901) *George Muller: all things are possible*. Reprint, Belfast: Ambassador Publications, 1999.

Pollock, J. (1963) *Moody without Sankey*. Reprint, London: Hodder and Stoughton Ltd, 1966.

Pollock, J. (1973) *Whitefield the evangelist*. Reprint, Eastbourne: Kingsway Publications, 2000.

Pollock, J. (1985) *Shaftesbury the reformer*. Reprint, Eastbourne: Kingsway Publications, 2000.

Pollock, J. (1989) *Wesley the preacher*. Reprint, Eastbourne: Kingsway Publications, 2000.

Rigg, J. (1891) *The living Wesley*. 2nd edn. London: Charles H. Kelly.

Robinson, W. S (2012) *Muckraker: the scandalous life and times of W T Stead, Britain's first investigative journalist*. Hull: Robson Press.

Rosell, G.M. and Dupuis, R.A.G. (ed.) (1989) *The memoirs of Charles Finney*. Grand Rapids: Zondervan Publishing House.

Salvation Army Heritage Centre, London.

Schama, S. (1989) *Citizens: a chronicle of the French revolution*. London: Penguin Group.

Schama, S. (2002) *A history of Britain: volume 3 the fate of empire 1776-2000*. London: BBC Worldwide Ltd.

Schama, S. (2005) *Rough crossings: Britain, the slaves and the American revolution*. Reprint, London: Vintage, 2009.

Schlicke, P. (1999) *The Oxford companion to Charles Dickens*. Oxford: Oxford University Press.

Semmel, B. (1974) *The Methodist revolution*. London: Heinemann Educational Books Ltd.

Sewel, W. (2010) *The history of the rise, increase, and progress of the Christian people called Quakers: intermixed with several remarkable occurrences*. Toronto: Gale ECCO.

Smithyman, A.B. (2013) Collected audio / written archives.

Stowell-Brown, et al. (1877) *The day of rest: illustrated journal of Sunday reading*. London: Strahan and Company Ltd.

Sumrall, D. (1995) *Pioneers of faith*. Oklahoma, Harrison House Inc.

Telford, J. (1902) *John Wesley: into all the world*. Reprint, Belfast: Ambassador Publications, 1999.

Tomalin, C. (2011) *Charles Dickens: a life*. London: Penguin Books.

Torrey, R.A. (1903) *Revival addresses*. London: Flemming H. Revell Company.

Torrey, R.A. (1955) *How to pray*. London: Oliphants Ltd.

Tozer, A.W. (2005) *The radical cross: living the passion of Christ*. Reprint, Pennsylvania: Wing Spread Publishers, 2009.

Tozer, A.W. (2009) *Reclaiming Christianity: a call to authentic faith*. Ventura: Regal.

Vipont, E. (1975) *George Fox and the valiant sixty*. London: Hamish Hamilton Ltd.

Ward, C. (1973) *Anarchy in action*. Reprint, London: Freedom Press, 2001.

Wardle, Irving: *Hair in London*. The London Times, 27 Sept 1969. Websource http://news.bbc.co.uk/onthisday/hi/dates/stories/september/27/newsid_3107000/3107815.stm.

The Way, 2010. Film. Directed by Emilio Estevez. USA: Filmax and Elixir Films.

Wesley, J (1872) *The works of John Wesley*. London: Wesleyan Methodist Book Room.

Wesley, J. (1831) *The works of reverend John Wesley, A.M: sometime fellow of Lincoln College, Oxford*. New York: J. Emory and B. Waugh.

Wilder, T. (1928) *The angel that troubled the waters: and other plays*. New York: Coward and McCann.

Wright, N.T. (2004) *The New Testament and the people of God*. 7th edn. London: Society For Promoting Christian Knowledge.